Restoring Convertibles

Restoring Convertibles

FROM RAGS TO RICHES

Burt Mills

Illustrated

DODD, MEAD & COMPANY
NEW YORK

1 2 3 4 5 6 7 8 9 10

Library of Congress Cataloging in Publication Data

Mills, Burt.
    Restoring convertibles.

    Bibliography: p.
    Includes index.
    1. Automobiles—Restoration.   I. Title.
TL152.2.M55   629.28′8′22   77-21351
ISBN 0-396-07382-4

This book is
affectionately dedicated
to my wife
PAT,
to my son
TONY,
who took many of the pictures,
and to all who have
fond memories of
convertibles.

Acknowledgments

Acknowledgment is gratefully made to the following, who either furnished some of the pictures used in this book or allowed photographs of their cars to be taken on their premises:

Jere DeBacker, Boulder, Colorado
Hall-Kraft Products, Denver, Colorado
David Kerr, Denver, Colorado
Soneff's Classic Auto Sales, Denver, Colorado

Preface

In this book you'll find information that will be helpful in restoring a post-World War II convertible to tip-top shape. Because information on mechanical repairs for these cars is readily available, this book doesn't cover engines, drive trains, suspension systems, brakes or steering. It is concerned with repairs peculiar to the convertible body.

Most of the pictures show convertibles in average condition—about as you'll find them—or in the process of being repaired, not as completely restored cars.

This book is written for the beginning restorer, man or woman, who is not necessarily mechanically inclined—it is for those who would like the fun of restoring and driving a convertible, and who would be pleased to know their investment is continually increasing in value.

Good luck!

Burt Mills

Contents

I | Choosing Your Convertible

II | Restoring Your Convertible

8 A COAT OF MANY COLORS 199

How to paint your convertible. Preparation of the
surface for painting. Masking, priming, etc. Color
scheme options available.

9 KEEP AMERICA BEAUTIFUL 209

Tips on keeping your convertible in showroom
condition once it is restored.

I

CHOOSING
YOUR
CONVERTIBLE

The last of its kind. After fifty years of "ragtops," the 1976 Cadillac Fleetwood Eldorado convertible became the last convertible produced by U.S. car makers.

1

An Endangered Species

Convertibles, once the epitome of dash, swank and verve, have been dropped by U.S. car manufacturers and join phaetons, town cars, and speedsters in the fascinating mural of past automotive body styles.

A favorite with the young and the young-at-heart, convertibles played an important role in the evolution of style in U.S. cars. The convertible gave a touch of class to car catalogs and drew people into showrooms. Convertibles made Chevrolets and Fords acceptable to many who were used to driving more expensive cars. Although convertibles usually were the most expensive models in the line, they found their way into the garages and hearts of millions of drivers. Memories of good times in convertibles still linger in the minds of many.

The convertible coupe evolved from the roadster, as manufacturers offered customers the comfort and convenience of roll-up windows instead of side curtains in a car with a folding roof.

Ford's first convertible coupe was the 1928 Model A, though there had been a "couplet" in the early T days. Ford continued the roadster until the end of its 1937 model run. Chevrolet offered its first convertible in 1928; its roadster was continued until the 1935 model. Plymouth presented a convertible coupe in 1929 and continued its roadster until 1934. The other car lines manufactured by Chrysler, Ford and General Motors all produced convertible coupes while phasing out roadsters over a period of years.

Early convertible coupes had but one bench seat, which would hold two or three persons. There was a rumble seat for additional passengers. Some custom-designed models late in the 1920s moved the second seat inside the car. This innovation was offered by Ford and Chevrolet in 1931, and by Plymouth the following year. Ford called theirs the A400. Chevrolet chose the name convertible victoria. Other manufacturers followed suit, calling their versions convertible victorias, convertible club coupes or convertible two-door sedans. The convertible coupe and the convertible two-door sedan body styles were combined within a few years, and the body style became known as the convertible club coupe through the years before World War II. Afterward they were usually known only as convertibles, or convertible coupes.

Some convertibles had only one window per side, usually with a wider door, as on the two-door sedans. The quarter section behind the door was covered with roofing material. By this time chrome landau bars had disappeared, and the top-operating mechanisms were on the inside. The Lincoln Continental convertible coupes of 1939 through 1948 are prime examples, as are the Ford convertible club coupes that appeared in 1936 and continued through the end of the 1941 model run. Ford added a second window per side with the 1942 models. General Motors and Chrysler followed this styling, as did the independents, Hudson, Nash, Packard, Studebaker and others.

The convertible four-door sedan evolved from the touring car, or phaeton. Customers preferred the convenience and comfort of a snug top and roll-up windows. Though far more expensive than touring cars, their style and comfort caught on, and the touring car faded away. Chevrolet's last touring car was produced in 1935, and Plymouth also discontinued the model that year. The last

Lincoln Continental produced the last four-door U.S. convertibles from 1961 through 1968, when a change in body construction ruled out the body style.

Ford phaeton was the 1938 model. Other Ford, Chrysler and General Motors lines phased out phaetons, and by Pearl Harbor Day, only convertible club coupes and convertible sedans were offered.

Convertibles never accounted for even 10 percent of the market. They carried a higher price tag, and most manufacturers didn't expect to sell many. The convertible sedan was dropped by established manufacturers after World War II due to shortages and escalating costs. Only Kaiser-Frazer revived the body style for a short period. It wasn't until the 1961 Lincoln Continental that a four-door convertible was again offered, lasting until 1968.

By 1972, sales of convertibles accounted for less than 1 percent of the market. Manufacturers couldn't keep the model in their lines, so one by one they dropped the convertible.

Some enthusiasts believe that if manufacturers had continued to offer distinctive convertibles styled like the cars of the 1930s and 1940s, there would still be a market. They refer to the beautiful convertible sedans offered by Auburn, Buick Limited, Cadillac V-12 and V-16, LaSalle, Lincoln, Marmon, Packard Super 8 and V-12, Pierce Arrow and Stutz. Many of these bodies were designed by such famous body designers as Bowman-Schwartz, Brunn, Darrin, Dietrich, Derham, Fleetwood, Judkins, LeBaron, Locke, Holbrook, Rollston, Willoughby and others. Some of these designs became production models after a year or two.

Convertible lovers mention convertible coupes such as the Auburn Speedsters, Cord 812's, Chrysler Highlander, Nash's "Special" convertible of 1940 with the cut-down door, Packard's Darrin Custom 180's of 1940 and 1941, and the Lincoln Continental convertibles. As evidence that really distinctive convertibles are in demand, they point to fiberglass replicas being produced of the Auburn and Cord.

Those who mourn the passing of the convertible note the success of some foreign marques, such as the Jaguar, MG and Triumph from England and the Mercedes from Germany. However, this "success" is questionable, since Jaguar discontinued their drophead E-type car. Triumph is offering only dressed-up versions of two cars that are several years old, their current TR-7 being a hardtop. The Mercedes body style has been offered a few years, and is priced far above what most people can or will pay for a car.

Really distinctive convertibles disappeared when the postwar bodies were designed. The few that were in production in 1941 and 1942 were offered in the first postwar lines but weren't included when new bodies were designed. The market for convertibles had dropped to the point where it wasn't economically feasible to design, manufacture and market a truly different convertible body style. Aside from some "show cars" that were put into limited production after World War II, most convertibles were hardtop models with altered windshield framing, some body or frame stiffening, and the convertible top and its operating mechanism substituted for the metal top.

Time has taken its toll of pre-World War II convertibles. They're now mighty scarce, and command very high prices. Most post-World War II convertibles, while not as distinctive as those that preceded them, are competent cars. They'll keep up with today's cars on the freeways and in traffic. Many have automatic transmissions, power brakes, power steering, power windows, power tops, and the other automatic devices to which we've become accustomed. These are cars you can drive every day if you wish. They make up in comfort and performance what they may lack in distinctiveness. Since they're still plentiful, prices are reasonable.

Convertibles are extinct; no more are being built. Cadillac turned out 14,000 Fleetwood Eldorado convertibles in 1976, re-

Graceful and sleek, the 1976 Cadillac Fleetwood Eldorado convertible offered the ultimate in luxury and comfort. Only minor trim changes were made during the last two years.

portedly because the company purchased that many tops. The other General Motors lines discontinued the convertible with the end of their 1975 model runs. Ford offered no convertible in their 1974 models, their last being the 1973 Cougar and Mustang. Chrysler turned out its last full-size convertible in 1970, and discontinued the body style in their smaller cars after 1971. American Motors dropped their Ambassador and Rambler convertibles with the 1967 model run and dropped the AMC Rebel in the 1968 model year.

Reasons for the demise of the convertible are many. Some consumer advocates harped on safety. In a roll-over accident, occupants belted in the car had to support the car's weight on their heads, necks and shoulders—not a happy thought. But if occupants weren't belted in, they were often thrown out of the car and the car rolled over on them.

Higher convertible prices, because of the extra labor required for finishing and fitting the convertible body, may have made the look-alike hardtop coupes more appealing to some people. The pillarless hardtop coupes (some people even called them hardtop convertibles) started showing up in 1948. By 1951 most manufacturers were offering the body style, often with exciting, exotic names.

Sleek lines, including many convertible styling features, made the lower price hardtops very popular. Chrysler hardtops may have lessened the demand for convertibles.

Development of a more leak-resistant sun roof offered many advantages of the convertible without some of the more obvious drawbacks. And increased demand for air-conditioned cars was probably another factor in the convertible's demise. Lack of insulation in convertible tops, and air leakage in and around the windows, made convertibles hard to air-condition properly. Higher maintenance costs may have been important too, since tops were expensive to repair and replace. The operating mechanisms for raising and lowering the tops often required adjustments and repairs.

Though snug when new, most convertibles became drafty and leak-prone after only a couple of years. The top material shrank, inviting drafts through the spaces over the windows. Anyone who has sat in a convertible after the car was parked in the sun for a few hours knows how hot and uncomfortable the upholstery can become.

These reasons combined to limit the demand for convertibles, and decreasing sales continued to drive up the price. In the final analysis, discontinuance of the convertible must be attributed mainly to high costs. Convertibles were another victim of inflation.

Like many other discontinued products, however, they will fast become collector's items, and their value (resale price) will increase.

Though it's hard to have your cake and eat it too, buying and restoring a post-World War II convertible is about as close as you can come to that delight. It's easy to have the fun of owning,

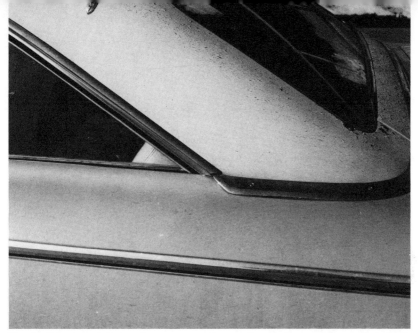

Ford Galaxie 500 hardtop coupe featured vinyl-covered roof (which cracked), including welting across top that simulated a convertible's rear roof bow.

Though only in production three years, Ford's retractable hardtop coupe heralded the approaching end of "ragtops." Metal top panels were hinged to fold when the top was lowered into the rear deck.

The tight fit of the convertible top on this Ford has kept the car quite snug and draft-free. Ford's last convertibles were large, well-finished cars, and able performers.

After only a few years top materials shrank, allowing leaks and drafts over windows and making convertibles somewhat uncomfortable at times.

"Hotter than Hell" was the comment often heard from people who sat on a convertible's seat after the car had been parked in the sun with the roof lowered.

There was plenty of luxury and style in mid-size GM convertibles, as evidenced by this Oldsmobile Cutlass. Body shell was shared with Buick, Chevrolet and Pontiac with skin and trim changes.

driving and restoring a convertible, and also to realize a substantial increase in the car's value the longer you keep it.

Nothing in the construction or design of a convertible should scare away the beginning restorer. Mechanically they're the same as other body styles of similar make, model and year. The body, lacking the rigidity provided by a solid top, usually is beefed up with extra bracing. Some manufacturers added an extra cross member to the frame.

Large plastic rear windows allowed ample back vision, making up for roof material stretched around the rear quarter, as on this Chrysler. Material often wrinkled with time.

Vinyl top on this Mustang has held up well, still fitting snugly around quarter window. Tops require minor attention and cleaning to keep them in proper condition.

Dodge Dart convertible offers sprightly performance in a small package. Easy to restore, it'll be worth more every year if kept in good condition.

Only minor trim changes were made on this 1950 Ford, which closely resembles the 1949 and 1951 models. Ford's first post-war body style featured slab sides. These models are popular among restorers and are still plentiful.

Chevrolet used the same body shell from 1949 through 1951. Easy to restore, they're rugged, dependable and good performers. There is no difficulty obtaining replacement parts.

Fake landau bars and vinyl roof covering give convertible look to Thunderbird hardtop. This may have helped the demise of convertibles.

General Motors creased metal roofs to simulate roof bows and used a vinyl covering to give the appearance of a convertible.

Trim parts and some interior components on convertibles may differ somewhat from hardtops, but offer no real problems to the restorer. Replacement tops are readily available for most makes. These can also be made quite easily by the novice restorer on a home sewing machine for a fraction of the cost of the ready-made replacement.

Convertibles of the mid to late 1940s and 1950s are now at the lowest prices they'll hit. The convertibles of the 1960s aren't apt to go much lower than current prices. Some dealers, realizing the demand for late-model convertibles, have already started to pay more attention to the few models produced during the 1970s, and it is unlikely that prices on these cars will drop appreciably.

The folding tops that made convertibles so desirable were also their Achilles' heel. As the tops wore, water leaked inside, damaging upholstery and causing rust-outs on lower body panels and floors. Many convertibles look in such rough condition after a few years they are often sold "as is," or consigned to wrecking yards years in advance of other body styles in their age bracket. In fact, the tattered condition of the top and upholstery may have turned off prospective buyers, making these models even better buys for the person who really wants to restore a convertible.

Now is the time to locate the convertible you'd like to own, before prices go any higher. Choose your convertible while they're still plentiful, and while new replacement parts and parts cars are easily obtainable.

2

The Choice Is Yours

The cars produced immediately following World War II were really only dressed-up 1941 and 1942 models. This was all the planning the industry could do in their rush to get cars back into dealers' showrooms. The first real postwar cars started showing up in late 1946 and 1947, and by 1949 all were in production.

Though cars were in terrific demand during these years, shortages of materials plaguing some manufacturers resulted in lower than planned production. Also, the first round of wage increases was felt in both the automotive supply and manufacturing industries. Strikes and work stoppages during the late 1940s increased prices and lowered production. These conditions culminated in the 1950s, forcing the consolidation of several companies and the end of others.

Nash merged with Hudson to form American Motors, and shortly after the merger Hudson disappeared. Studebaker and Packard joined forces, resulting in a Packard of much lower quality before it was finally discontinued in 1958. Studebaker continued as a marque for a time, but gave up the ghost shortly after moving auto production to Canada in the early 1960s. Kaiser-Frazer bit the dust in 1955. Willys dropped from the scene, with American Motors picking up the Jeep line.

The Big Three also had some casualties. Ford bombed on both the Edsel and Mark II Continental. Chrysler dropped the DeSoto. General Motors discontinued the Corvair. GM also confused the scene by bringing more standardization to their lines, yet giving new names and model designations to cars that were practically identical.

During these years the sale of foreign cars jumped tremendously, weakening the financial position of the companies least able to take the strain. The early 1960s stimulated the highly competitive battle in which Ford, Chrysler and General Motors tightened their grip on the market, forcing out every other manufacturer except American Motors.

During this era most manufacturers offered some convertible models. By and large they were good cars, well worth the investment of time and money necessary to restore them.

You can take your choice of the following: large or small, deluxe or standard, high-performance or economy models, sports cars, personal cars, or a few high-priced, limited-production models— all convertibles.

BUICK produced a wide range of convertibles from Supers to Roadmasters, starting in 1946. These were large, fast cars with the slope of the front fender carrying across the door and body to where the rear fender started. They had two windows per side, and the tops folded very flat into a well behind the seat. Buick's new body shell for 1949 was their first with the famous "portholes." The Riviera hardtop was introduced in 1949, which may have hastened the end of Buick convertibles. The 1950 Buicks had some chrome added, along with a model designated "Special," a smaller car. The vertical bars on the grilles were mounted as bumper guards, giving a very toothy grin to the front. The same model designations continued through 1951 and 1952. The Sky-

Horizontal lines and restrained use of chrome enhance the front of this Buick Electra. Massive appearance is coupled with able performance, making it a most desirable convertible.

lark was introduced with the 1953 models, a sleek, high-styled convertible with a chrome spear motif on each side.

With the 1954 cars Buick added the Century line. The Skylark convertible was changed considerably, with a tapering rear deck and bold chrome-plated taillights jutting from the fenders. The Skylark wasn't offered in 1956, 1957 or 1958. Convertibles were offered in all the other Buick lines, and the Limited was added in 1958.

In 1959 completely redesigned body shells featured chrome moldings that started over twin headlights and swept back and down to the center of a large taillight. Canted chrome-trimmed fins started with the vent windows in the front doors. Electra became the top of the line, with Invicta and LeSabre priced below it. Quite different styling was featured on the 1960 lines, with sculptured side panels, and a return of the portholes last seen in 1957; however, as they appeared on the 1960 models, they were highly stylized. The Electra convertible of 1960 featured a wide plated band along the bottoms of the fenders, doors and body panels, above the rocker panel strip.

The smaller Special and Special Skylark, completely different from its predecessor, was introduced in 1961 as Buick's compact car. As with all other Buick convertibles, many components were shared with other GM cars.

Buick continued to produce beautiful convertibles through the 1960s, ranging from their compact Special to the huge Electra 225. Styling became less flamboyant at the turn of the 1970s when the Centurion joined the line.

All Buick convertibles are excellent cars, and about as easy to restore as any you can choose. The 1954 Skylark is by far the most sought-after Buick convertible. The Electra 225 convertibles of the late 1960s are fast becoming favorites because of their size, luxury and performance.

CADILLAC offered convertibles in their Series 61 and 62 cars of 1946, and continued basically the same cars in 1947. Large and able, these good-looking cars helped push Cadillac into the No. 1 sales slot in the high-price field. Long pontoon-style front fenders

Cadillac's famous fins as they first appeared, starting a styling trend that lasted over a decade. Though absolutely no functional value, they did hide the gas tank filler pipe. Large ends on bumper helped protect fenders.

Cadillac Eldorado Biarritz, a show stopper, has become a collector's item. Sculptured metal at the rear continued the body line, and dual exhausts ran through the bumpers.

accented by a chrome midstrip continued back into the front doors. Tasteful chrome trim accented the car's size. Beautiful leather interiors made these convertibles real prizes. New body shells in 1948 blended the fender line into the body, offering a wider, sleeker car. The famous Cadillac "fins" first appeard on the 1948 cars. Cadillac retained the same body shell for 1949, but started their hardtop Coupe DeVille. The Series 62 Cadillac convertible of 1949 is a highly prized model, worth searching out.

The Eldorado convertible appeared in 1953, with the industry's first wrap-around windshield. It sported chrome-plated wire wheels, and was a knockout. Tail fins became huge with the 1957 model, and the Eldorado Biarritz was offered to compete with Lincoln's Continental Mark II. Rear-end styling of the Eldorado Biarritz featured exhaust pipes extending through bumper panels, with the center portion of the rear deck continuing to the bottom of the car unprotected by a bumper in the midsection.

Eldorado continued to be the top of the line for Cadillac, and their convertibles were spectacular cars, as easy to handle and fun to drive as they were beautiful. The Fleetwood name plate was attached to some of the models, indicating a more expensive interior trim and more external chrome.

As Cadillac purred through the 1960s, their long, low convertibles made many heads turn. The DeVille convertibles of 1963 and 1964 seem to be in considerable demand because of their clean styling. The Eldorado Biarritz of 1963 is highly prized. If you want a prestige convertible with plenty of class, choose a Cadillac. The Eldorado Biarritz of 1953 is the most desirable, closely followed by the Eldorado Biarritz of 1957 and 1958. They'll be expensive, but worth it.

CHEVROLET faced the World War II market with the Fleetline and Sportsmaster in 1946. These were facelifts of their successful

Tidy front-end treatment of Chevrolet's first real postwar models blended fender and hood line. Wrap-around bumper followed the curve of the grille. These models are deservedly popular to restore.

Chrome trim on rear fenders and top of fin mark dramatic styling of the 1957 Chevrolet. This fine-performing model can hold its own against larger, more powerful convertibles.

1942 models. Peppy and economical to drive, they were solidly built convertibles. In 1947 the Fleetline name was added to the line, as were some external chrome strips on the base of the fenders. The strips were continued in the 1948 cars. The first real postwar bodies appeared in the Styleline convertibles of 1949, an immediate hit. Continued virtually unchanged through 1952, these attractive, well-built convertibles made a lot of buyers happy. The Bel-Air first appeared in 1952, then sported a new body in 1953 which carried over into the 1954 lines.

New bodies with wrap-around windshields appeared in 1955, along with a zippy new V-8 engine. The 210 series and Delray were added to the line. Little change was made to the body shell during 1956 and 1957, but two-tone paint jobs and different chrome trim highlighted each year.

Starting to show signs of age, this Chevrolet Impala has been fitted with fancy wheel covers and mirrors on front fenders. The model is well worth restoring.

Fiberglass body plus many advanced mechanical features have made early Corvettes very popular. Both solid and cloth tops were furnished along with many optional extras.

New, larger bodies emphasizing low horizontal lines made the 1958 models an instant success. Chevrolet introduced the Impala line of stylish convertibles that held the top-of-the-line position through the end of Chevrolet's convertible production.

The Corvair was introduced in 1960. This small rear-engine car was offered in a convertible model too, and lasted until bad publicity almost equaling a vendetta drove it off the market in 1969. The Chevy II and Nova were introduced in 1962, indicating Chevrolet's recognition of the demand for smaller cars. Their mid-size Chevelle followed in 1964.

The Corvette, introduced by Chevrolet in 1953, fast became an entirely different machine than other Chevrolets. Sporting a fiberglass body, it has won wide acclaim for performance and style. Of the Chevrolet-produced convertibles, the Corvette is first choice for performance, and the Corvair is desirable for its rear engine and distinctive styling. All of Chevrolet's postwar convertibles are interesting cars, easy to restore. The 1955 through 1957 cars are the best performers of the regular line, and enjoy the most popularity.

CHRYSLER produced their New Yorker, Windsor and the wood-trimmed model Town and Country starting in 1946. These are large, well-engineered cars, somewhat less stylish than the cars of competing manufacturers. New bodies appeared with the 1949 cars, again featuring the New Yorker, Windsor and Town and Country convertibles (the Town and Country line was discontinued after 1950). Longer and lower, they were immediate successes, and the addition of the Saratoga and Newport lines added to their appeal. Bodies were virtually unchanged through 1954, with only minor trim changes from year to year.

New high-styled bodies with wrap-around windshields appeared in 1955, featuring two-tone paint jobs that accentuated the car's low lines. The convertibles were very handsome, with careful attention to upholstery and interior details. In the same year Chrysler's high-performance 300's bowed in, less bulky than the top-of-the-line Imperial, which was designated as a separate marque in 1954. The Crown, LeBaron and Southampton names were added

Dummy spare tire mounted on deck lid of Chrysler 300 gives a racy appearance. The 300 series, one of the most desirable Chryslers, offered high-performance cars with plenty of style.

Chrysler New Yorker featured a horizontal chrome strip along top of the fender line to accent car's length. Chryslers are easy to restore because of interchangeability of parts.

to the line, and the Windsor and New Yorker convertibles were continued. The 300 series developed into real muscle cars. They are the most desirable Chrysler convertibles, unless you want a huge car that will hold its own with any Cadillac, Lincoln or Packard. In that case, the Crown Imperial of 1964 would be an excellent choice.

CROSLEY offered a two-cylinder mini-car a few years before World War II, then changed to a four-cylinder engine with its postwar cars in 1947: a four-passenger convertible with fixed window frames (first used on the Ford A400) and a two-passenger open roadster named "Hotshot." The varnished wooden bows that held the convertible's roof in position were hand-placed in notches in the rail over the window and door, and were stored behind the rear seat when the roof was lowered. A new grille and minor front-end styling changes were added to the 1949 models, along with a slight extension of the rear deck. These models were carried over into 1950. A small spinner, with a miniature propeller, graced the 1951 and 1952 cars. Crosleys, discontinued in 1952, offer minimal transportation at minimal expense. Because of their scarcity they have a certain value.

DESOTO abandoned concealed headlights featured on their 1942 models when they introduced their 1946 cars. A four-window, two-door convertible was offered in their Custom line. These cars used many body stampings seen on other Chrysler-built cars, with the front fender flowing into about the middle of the front door, and rather stubby rear fenders. A new Custom convertible was introduced in 1949 with longer lines and a better balance between front- and rear-end styling. Only minor changes were made for 1950. Both a six- and an eight-cylinder convertible were offered in 1951, with a newly styled grille, bumper and other trim. A Sportsman Hardtop was offered, which must have competed with their convertibles. The cars remained much the same through 1954, when the Coronado and Firedome names were used.

The 1955 models were real knockouts, beautifully styled with a dramatic spear motif on the sides of the Fireflite and Fireflite Adventurer convertibles. Fins showed up on the 1956 models, and the

Golden Adventurer sported elaborate three-lens taillights with huge chrome bumper ends below them. The 1957 models carried most of the same sheet metal, but with a two-piece grille containing a large airscoop. Also, the fins were enlarged, the taillights were changed and the exhausts protruded through the rear bumper. The 1958 and 1959 models are very similar. The Adventurer featured chrome luggage strips on the rear deck, plus a divided front seat with a swivel base on the passenger's side.

The 1960 model year saw new, larger bodies with large fins that actually started just ahead of the front door handle. A large mesh grille rose from a massive slightly V-shaped bumper. More attractive, less fussy taillights gave a better appearance to the rear. The same bodies, with a slightly different grille, graced the short-lived 1961 models. Since DeSoto discontinued production in 1961, any convertible of that year would have considerable value because of scarcity. The 1955 convertibles are the most desirable because of their clean styling, the 1959s because of their extra features. The restorer can count on most body components from other Chrysler-built cars fitting DeSotos as replacements.

DODGE first offered their Custom Luxury Liners in 1941. These cars were face-lifted for 1946, continuing with next to no changes

Showing signs of wear and neglect, this Dodge Coronet needs only minor body work, a new top and cosmetic attention. Convertibles in similar condition often sell for less than other body styles.

through the 1948 model run. They are good-looking, easy-to-restore cars. In 1949, in addition to the Coronet line in which an attractive convertible was offered, Dodge introduced a lower-priced Wayfarer roadster with a manually-operated top. This two-passenger car was produced for three model years. The Diplomat series joined the line in 1950, and only minor styling changes were made in the 1951 and 1952 Diplomat models.

Different body shells appeared in 1953, when the Meadowbrook first came on the scene. The Coronet convertible featured a rear-mounted spare wheel as an option. Dodge added the Royal line in 1954: larger, lower cars with clean styling. Narrow chrome molding ran from above the front wheel arch across the door, curving down to meet a chrome gravel guard at the front of the rear wheel arch, then continuing across the rear fender and ending under the taillight.

Two- and three-tone color schemes accentuated the 1956 styling, when the first wrap-around windshield appeared on Dodge's Custom Royal convertible. Only minor changes were offered for 1957 and 1958. The 1959 model year saw a different treatment for the rear fins, along with grille and bumper changes in front. In 1960 Dodge introduced the Polara, an attractive car despite its large rear fins. The fin treatment was drastically changed in 1961 when new side moldings brought the whole design together. Until closely examined, the concave grille looked as if it had been dented.

The compact Dodge Lancer, introduced in 1961, continued with only minor trim changes through 1962.

The 1962 model year brought more style changes, making the Polara a neater looking package. The Polara 500 convertible was added in 1963, featuring low horizontal taillights and exceptionally sleek, clean styling. This continued in the 1964 models, and was typical of Dodge styling in 1965 and the remaining years that the company produced a convertible.

The Dodge Dart series was introduced in 1960 as their small car, and later included the Phoenix, 440, GT and 270 convertibles. These are all easy to restore, as many parts exchange with other Chrysler Corporation cars. The 1955 and 1956 Custom Royal Lancer convertibles seem to be the most popular as restoration choices, with the Polaras of the early 1960s a close second. The 1963 Dart GT is the most desirable of the small models.

EDSEL, sharing both Ford and Mercury components with its own distinctive variations, could be purchased as a Corsair or Citation convertible beginning in 1958. The 1958 cars featured a more distinctive and attractive radiator grille than the 1959s, causing one television comedian to claim the 1959 Edsel looked like an Oldsmobile that had sucked on a lemon. Edsels had numerous interior refinements that endeared them to many. Discontinued early in the 1960 model run, they are fast becoming collectors' items. The Citation convertible was the more expensive model. Choose either the 1958 Citation because of its unique grille, or the 1960 because of the small production. Beware of counterfeit Edsels made out of Fords.

FORD produced a Super Deluxe and a wood-trimmed Sportsman convertible in 1946. These were basically the 1942 car. Their first postwar convertible body, called a Custom, appeared in the 1949 lineup. These were the slab-sided Fords, very attractive, with a host of features unheard of on previous Fords. With only minor changes to the grille and other trim, the body style was continued through the end of the 1951 model run. Continental kits, allowing the spare wheel to be mounted outside the squared-off rear deck, were a popular option, as was a custom top that covered the second window, leaving a wide expanse of top material behind the door window.

The Sunliner appeared in 1952, a larger convertible than its predecessor. It continued with only minor trim changes through 1954. The Crestline convertibles introduced in 1952 and continued through 1954 were clean-lined cars, in heavy demand today. In 1955 Ford added a wrap-around windshield and two-tone color schemes, separated by a chrome spear motif that featured the Ford crest on the front door. Few other changes were made in 1955. In 1956 the Skyliner, a hardtop coupe with a plexiglass insert in the roof, caused quite a sensation and may have taken some buyers away from the true convertibles. New bodies for 1957 and 1958 were larger and heavier looking. The Skyliner became

A 1946 Ford convertible being readied for a needed paint job. Minor
dings and dents on its sound body have been straightened and filled, ready
for priming. Chrome trim has been removed from the grille.

Clean rear deck styling on 1950 Fords explains why these cars have remained popular over the years. Some buyers added a rear-mounted spare
tire to give a "continental" touch.

the Fairlane 500 Skyliner with a retractable steel roof, the first hardtop convertible. This was continued through 1959.

The graceful curved styling of the 1960 Sunliner convertible has made it a most desirable car. In 1961 the Galaxie convertible stole the show; a few trim changes, made for the 1962 models, kept it popular. The Galaxie 500 XL models appeared in 1964 and 1965. Ford styling continued with more sleek-looking convertibles as the 1960s turned to the 1970s.

The Falcon came on the scene in 1960 to compete in the small-car field. Later this was offered as the Falcon Sprint and the Falcon Futura. The sporty Mustang, produced by Ford, made its debut in 1964. These stylish little convertibles offered a GT model in 1965, and continued through 1973.

Ford claims to have dominated the convertible field for many years, and their convertibles have always enjoyed tremendous popularity. They are fun to restore and fun to drive. The wood-trimmed Sportsman convertibles of 1946 and 1947 are the most sought-after because of their sporty appearance and scarcity. The retractable hardtops of 1957, 1958 and 1959 are in demand as the only true hardtop convertibles produced in the U.S. Front-end

Recessed headlights and side grilles were front-end styling features of Ford convertibles. Small dent and missing chrome behind the door are minor, and a beginning restorer could easily make repairs.

styling has made the 1960 Sunliner a favorite among collectors, as are the last years of the Galaxie XL's. You can't go wrong on any year or model Ford-built convertible.

HUDSON, while still an independent, offered the Commodore, Pacemaker and Hornet convertibles. Hudson offered both six- and eight-cylinder convertibles. Their 1946 and 1947 models were face-lifted prewar cars. Hudson introduced their first real postwar cars in late 1947, as 1948 models. These cars, with their "step-down" design, stressed performance and safety. Their good looks and careful finishing have made them very desirable. No convertible was offered in the Jet line of compacts.

Plated wheel covers giving the appearance of wire wheels were popular in the 1950s, as on this Hudson Hornet. In many cases chrome parts can be scoured and restored to original luster with strong detergent solution, making plating unnecessary.

Massive and low, Hudson featured "step-down" styling on its first postwar models. These very solid cars have stood up well, and because of high performance they are in considerable demand.

After Hudson's merger with Nash to form American Motors, Hudson convertibles were no longer offered, other than a nameplate and hubcaps put on a few Ramblers and the sub-compact Metropolitans that Nash was producing. Hudson lost its identity in 1955, 1956 and 1957, when sharing the Nash body shell, and was discontinued after the 1957 model run.

Because of their high performance, styling and careful finishing, Hudson convertibles from 1948 through 1954 are in demand and are a good investment.

KAISER-FRAZER offered a four-door convertible sedan in both makes in their first body shell of 1947 through 1949, and continued producing these convertibles using the older body shell when their other models were redesigned in 1950. No convertible coupes were offered, and no convertibles were available in the compact Henry J line. A few specially bodied Kaiser-Darrin two-passenger convertibles, with sliding doors, were produced in 1954 and 1955. Because of their rarity, any Kaiser or Frazer convertible is a good investment.

LINCOLN continued their famous Continental convertibles through the end of the 1948 model run. These sleek, high-styled luxury cars are perhaps the most sought-after convertibles, never on the market long before someone snaps them up. Lincoln also produced a convertible coupe in their regular line, known as the Zephyr before World War II. But the Zephyr name was dropped, and from 1946 through 1948 these V-12's were simply called Lincolns. These convertibles are extremely rare as so few were produced.

With the 1949 models Lincoln offered two lines: the Lincoln and the Lincoln Cosmopolitan. The Lincoln shared some body components with Mercury in the years through 1951, but the Cosmopolitan models had a completely different body. Both convertibles during these years were high-performance cars with quality construction and finishing. In 1952 new bodies were offered, and the Cosmopolitan and Capri used the same bodies. The convertibles of 1952 through 1955 are scarce, for not many were produced. Only minor trim changes in the grilles and front bumpers and taillight treatment differentiate the four model years of these very attractive cars.

With the 1956 models the Cosmopolitan line was dropped and replaced by the Premiere. Capri was continued, and both models

This four-door Continental convertible is in about average condition. Though these cars are complicated from a mechanical standpoint, their high quality and sophisticated styling make them very desirable.

used the same body shell. Both were continued in 1957 with only minor trim changes. These large cars have horizontal chrome trim placed low on the body to accentuate the length. The exhaust pipes extend through the bumpers with a heavy chrome deflector.

The Mark II Continental was offered in 1956 and again the following year. These were very expensive cars turned out in small quantities, supposedly after potential buyers had been screened to be sure they were the kind of people the company thought should have these fine automobiles. Competing in this market were the Cadillac Eldorado Biarritz and the Packard Caribbean on the domestic market, and the Rolls Royce and Mercedes on the import market. The Mark II's were two-door hardtop coupes, but a few convertibles were produced by the Derham Body Company, which modified the basic Mark II body shell.

The Continental surfaced again as a body style only in the Lincoln line for 1958, as Capri, Premiere and Continental Mark III lines were offered. These convertibles were very large cars, long, low and wide. They featured a roof that was completely hidden by a metal panel when lowered. The reverse slant of the rear roof line gave them a distinctive appearance, and a large rear window. They continued with only minor trim changes through the 1960 model run. These are very desirable cars because of their size and styling.

Starting with the 1961 models, all Lincolns had monocoque body construction and were called Continentals. They were smaller, trimmer cars, with exceptionally clean lines. A smartly styled four-door convertible sedan was offered through the 1968 model run, with only minor changes during the intervening years. These luxurious, high-powered cars were beautifully made and finished. They are complicated machines, but worth the restoration effort since they are the last U.S.-built four-door convertibles. Prices on the 1961 through 1968 Lincoln Continental convertibles reached their low point in 1974 and have been climbing ever since, proving their desirability to the collector-restorer. No convertibles were offered by Lincoln after the 1968 model run, either in their regular lines or the Mark IV models.

MERCURY was a big Ford when first introduced and offered

in prewar days. Immediately after World War II the prewar bodies were dressed up a bit. They were offered in 1946 and 1947 in both a convertible coupe and a wood-trimmed Sportsman convertible. New bodies, sharing some Lincoln components, were introduced in 1949; only minor trim changes were made in 1950 and 1951. These were large cars with able performance and good attention to finishing. Production was high on these popular models, so quite a few are still available.

New bodies appeared in 1952. Both Custom and Monterey lines were offered, resembling slightly scaled-down Lincolns. Clean and lithe, the body shell was used through the 1954 model run. In 1955 the Sun Valley appeared, a hardtop coupe with a plexiglass roof insert similar to Ford's Skyliner. New bodies with wrap-around windshields sold in 1955, with bold chrome side trim. Dual headlights plus grille and bumper changes, along with different rear fenders and taillights, marked the 1957 models. A Turnpike Cruiser hardtop coupe was introduced in 1957, to compete with the Monterey and Montclair convertibles. Only slight styling changes were made for the 1958 lines.

New, longer bodies were designed for the 1959 cars and carried over in the 1960 lines. The Monterey convertible of 1960 is a standout for clean styling, and is minus some extraneous chrome trim offered on the higher priced Park Lane. Slightly smaller bodies graced the 1961 models; minor chrome trim changes were made for the 1962 models. Convertibles of both years are good-looking cars. With the 1963 models, the S-55 became the top-of-the-line convertible. This large, roomy car has tasteful chrome trim and restrained styling.

Redesigned for 1965, both Monterey and Park Lane were big cars with clean styling. As continued in 1966, the Park Lane convertible is one of the most desirable Mercury convertibles. Only trim changes and slight style modifications were made in 1967.

Mercury's compact Comet, which appeared in 1960, shared many body stampings with the Ford Falcon, just as Mercury's Cougar convertible shared many Mustang body stampings. Mercury's last convertible was the 1973 Cougar, which by this time had grown considerably and could no longer be considered a small car.

The 1946–47 Mercury Sportsman convertible is the most valuable because of its scarcity. The sleek 1966 Park Lane will probably remain the most "wanted" of the Mercury line.

NASH offered a "Special" convertible in their prewar cars, a racy model with cut-down doors, but didn't revive this most attractive body when they resumed production in 1946. The Ambassador convertible was larger and lacked the grace of the "Special." It was continued through the 1948 model run. Not many were sold, so the first postwar Nash convertibles are now in demand because of their scarcity. With new bodies in 1949, Nash dropped convertibles in their full-size cars. These were the bulbous cars with the covered-front wheels, sometimes dubbed "highway schmoo's." In 1950 Rambler was offered as a small six-cylinder convertible with fixed window frames and roof rail. The Country Club models of 1951 and 1952 offered a rear-mounted spare. The Custom and Country Club Ramblers were continued through the end of the 1955 model run, when Ramblers became much larger.

The Metropolitan, a sub-compact with an Austin engine, was

A true economy car, AMC's Rambler is easy to repair and will give good service for years. Some paint, minor straightening and wheel discs would work wonders with this car's appearance. Ramblers are now scarce.

A real sub-compact, Nash Metropolitan was a two-seater. Covered front wheels matched styling of other Nash lines. These well-built little cars are in demand because of their scarcity and uniqueness.

offered as a convertible from 1955 through 1960, when price increases brought it into competition with the Rambler American.

After Nash merged with Hudson to form American Motors, the Ambassador became the top-of-the-line. Rambler's American convertible was continued with trim changes through 1967. The Classic line of cars offered a convertible with few changes in the 1964–67 lines. The last Ambassador convertible was available in the 1967 model run, and the last AMC convertible was the AMC Rebel in 1968. Production of Nash and later AMC convertibles was never high, and the few remaining have attained considerable value because of their scarcity. At the right price they are good buys for the beginner-restorer.

OLDSMOBILE was a style leader as the world headed into World War II. The company's beautiful convertibles were offered in both six- and eight-cylinder models in 1946, with only minor styling changes. The six-cylinder was called Model 66, and the eight-cylinder Model 98. New, longer, wider bodies were introduced in 1949 and were continued with minor trim changes through 1952. The convertibles of these years were stylish cars with able performance. They are excellent candidates for the restorer, as many of the body stampings were similar to those GM used on Chevrolet, Buick and Pontiac.

New bodies were fitted in 1953, as the Super 88 and Holiday 98 models. Few changes were necessary in 1954 or 1955, with the exception of the wrap-around windshield added in 1955. Many

Clean styling has kept this Oldsmobile convertible an attractive car. Minor dent behind the front wheel cutout isn't difficult to repair. Oldsmobiles share many body components with other GM lines.

changes were made in 1957, when the Golden Rocket and Starfire joined the model lines. In 1958 changes appeared in the front fenders to accommodate double headlights and in the rear-end styling. What many consider excessive, unnecessary chrome trim was also applied. In 1959 and 1960 the 98 models continued as the top-of-the-line. The Starfire convertibles of 1961–63 were handsome cars, identified by bright metal or a contrasting color running in a bold panel from front to rear along the sides. These large convertibles continued with style and trim changes through the end of Oldsmobile's convertible production.

The compact Olds F-85, sharing many body components with the Buick Special, Chevrolet Nova and Pontiac Tempest, was first offered in 1961. Both large and small Oldsmobiles of the 1950s and 1960s are good cars, though some were overly ornamented with chrome. The 1964 Olds F-85 Cutlass convertible stands out among the compact cars. The 1961 Starfire convertible seems to be the most desirable of the large Oldsmobiles.

PACKARD, America's No. 1 luxury car in the 1930s, offered a wide variety of convertibles in 1942, including the 110, a six-cylinder car; the 120, a medium-priced eight; the large 180 series; and a Darrin Custom 180 with cut-down doors and truly advanced styling for its day. Their first postwar convertibles were in the Super 8 and Custom 8 series, very similar to the prewar cars. There were continued with the new body styles offered in 1948. These models, often referred to as the "pregnant Packards," were excellent cars, but their slab-sided styling wasn't overly popular. Only minor trim changes were made in the 1950 models.

The 1951 models offered new, very attractive styling, with a Mayfair 250, a 300 series, and a 400 Patrician series. These were large, cleanly designed cars. Few changes were made in 1952 or 1953, when a top-of-the-line Caribbean convertible with a rear-mounted spare and many advanced styling features was offered as a limited-production car. The Caribbean was offered as a regular production model in 1954, though somewhat modified. The Deluxe and Caribbean convertibles continued through the end of regular Packard production in 1956. No convertibles were offered in the 1957 and 1958 lines, when some Packard styling was grafted on Studebakers. Packards as a separate marque were high-quality cars, well engineered and impeccably finished. Packard convertibles are a good investment. The 1953 Caribbean tops the list, closely followed by the 1954 model. The Mayfair convertible of 1953 offers the largest engine of the Packard line in a slightly smaller (though still large) car. The Custom 8's of 1948 and 1949 are a third choice.

PLYMOUTH was offering a Special Deluxe convertible before World War II, and continued essentially the same car in their 1946–48 lines. Though they lacked rear seat room, they were popular models. New, roomier bodies were offered in 1949, and the Special Deluxe convertible was good-looking. These six-cylinder cars were continued with only minor changes through the 1952 model run. New bodies in 1953 and 1954 were larger; both Belvedere and Cranbrook convertibles were available. A wrap-around windshield on new bodies gave the 1955 models more style, with the Belvedere convertible being top-of-the-line. Few changes were made in 1956 when the Fury models were introduced. In 1957 Plymouth added large fins to the rear fenders, and different front-end treatment necessitated by twin headlights. Constrasting color inserts on the side panels gave the cars a longer, lower appearance.

Few changes were made for 1958, but the stylists went all-out in 1959. The Fury convertible that year sported a dummy spare wheel mounted on the rear deck lid, as well as large chrome-trimmed fins. The following year only trim changes were made. In 1961 the fins disappeared as large, low bodies became the vogue. Bullet-shape taillights were grafted to the rear, and a grille resembling the head of an electric shaver made the Fury convertible a distinctive car. Styling was somewhat more subdued for the 1962 models, and this carried over the next two years. In 1965 Plymouth offered a more squared-off design, quite free of meaningless chrome, and such restraint marked Plymouth convertible styling of the late 1960s.

Plymouth introduced the smaller Valiant and Valiant Signet convertibles in 1960 to compete with the smaller cars offered by American Motors, Ford and General Motors. These attractively styled cars, economical yet peppy, are now very desirable.

Of Plymouth's large cars, the 1963 and 1964 Fury convertibles are the most wanted, while the 1965 Valiant Signet convertible is most desirable of the small Plymouths.

PONTIAC offered both six- and eight-cylinder convertibles in 1942. Their Torpedo styling was little changed in the 1946 and 1947 models, as both Torpedo and Deluxe Streamliner convertibles; they closely resembled other GM offerings of those years. Only minor trim changes were made for the 1948 models. However, with the new body styles in 1949, longer, lower and wider bodies graced the Deluxe Chieftan and Streamliner convertibles. The cars were practically unchanged the next three years. The Catalina model was introduced in 1952 and continued in 1953. Longer cars appeared in 1954, with the Chieftan and Star Chief Deluxe convertibles being very attractive.

A new V-8 engine gave the newly styled 1955 models extra power and performance. The Chieftan and Star Chief convertibles offered striking two-tone paint jobs and a choice of colorful vinyl interiors. Few changes were made for the 1956 lineup. In 1957 new, larger bodies were offered, with the Bonneville convertible becoming the top-of-the-line model. Double headlights and rear trim changes were the main differences for 1958, though bright metal and painted inserts on the sides were eye-catching.

More subdued styling was introduced on the 1958 models, with

Long rear deck of Pontiac Bonneville was a styling feature that appealed to many and gave huge storage space. Pontiacs are well-built cars, comparatively easy to restore and usually worth the time and money.

simulated vents on the rear fender hinting at a rear engine. This meaningless trim on the rear body panels, fenders and side trim was used by many stylists who for some reason tried to give the impression the car's engine was no longer forward. The story is told that Cadillac was toying with the idea of a rear-engined car, and these bolt-on trim parts were added on GM cars to test public reaction. As GM stylists decreed, other designers seemed to follow.

The 1960 and 1961 models were trim and attractive. Only slight changes were made in 1962. Bonneville and Grand Prix models topped the line—able and attractive convertibles. The 1964 models continued the split front grille used by Pontiac in 1959 but recessed the side panels, giving a very good-looking front appearance. The "Coke-bottle" side treatment, so typical of Pontiacs in the late 1960s, started with a modest bulge behind the front doors of the 1965 model.

Pontiac's Tempest was introduced in 1961, and the LeMans in 1962. The popular GTO's were first offered in 1964. Good looks and fine performance have made Pontiac convertibles restorers' favorites. The 1949 Streamliner heads the list, followed by the 1953 Star Chief among the large cars. The 1965 GTO seems the most popular of the small Pontiacs.

STUDEBAKER was offering convertibles in their Champion, Commander and President lines when World War II halted production. Their 1946 models were face-lifted 1942 models; Studebaker led the industry with the first truly new postwar cars in

43

Stubby appearance of Lark Daytona didn't help sales, even though its V-8 engine gave plenty of zip. Becoming scarce, these small Studebakers will appreciate rapidly in the years ahead.

May 1946, presented as 1947 models. The Champion and Commanders were crowd-stoppers, continuing virtually unchanged through the 1949 model run. A styling goof in 1950 grafted new front-end treatment featuring a large chrome hub at the front of the hood, above the grilles, that looked like the propeller hub on an airplane. Both six- and eight-cylinder convertibles were offered. The cars were little changed in 1951 when the Commander series was offered with a V-8 engine. Modifications to the front end, abandoning the large chrome hub, made the cars more attractive, though they were still using the body shell introduced in 1946.

New models appeared in 1953, but these didn't include a convertible. The streamlined Starliners would have made beautiful convertibles, but only one or two are known to have been rebuilt by custom body builders. The Lark series of compacts offered a sharp-looking convertible in both a six-cylinder and small V-8; because of rarity, they have considerable value. No convertible was offered in the high-styled, high-performance Avanti series. Studebaker produced their last cars from a plant in Canada in 1966.

THUNDERBIRD, at first largely built from Ford components but with some very distinctive body stampings, was introduced as a "personal" car in 1955. It was an immediate success and fast became a far different car. The 1955–57 models, two-passenger cars often called "Earlybirds," command high prices today, and a restorable car isn't for sale long. These were convertibles with a molded fiberglass top that could convert them into a snug coupe when desired.

New bodies in 1958 transformed the Thunderbird into a four-passenger car. These featured twin headlights, a squared-off trunk and a wrap-around windshield. The convertible was a separate model; a clamp-on top was no longer offered. Called "Square-birds" by those who really liked them, the car was offered with only minor trim changes through 1960. An optional rear-mounted spare wheel lengthened the rear overhang, making the car scrape on steep driveways.

The "Curvybird" appeared in 1961, a trimmer and less ornate design. A fiberglass tonneau with headrests was available to transform the car into a two-passenger model when the roof was lowered. This new body was in production with only minor trim changes through the 1963 model run, when it gave way to the 1964 cars, affectionately dubbed "Mightybirds" because of their powerful performance. These were well-designed models with a formal squared-off roof line. One of the hardtop models featured a

Thunderbirds from 1955 through 1957, small two-seaters, have become very much in demand. Rear-mounted spare and bumper extension were extras. Easy availability of Ford parts cuts restoration costs.

These fourth series T-birds aren't apt to go any lower in price. Well made and sporty in appearance, they're worth the time and expense of good restoration, and will appreciate quite rapidly.

vinyl-covered roof and one window per side, with fake landau bars, giving the appearance of a convertible. These were little changed for 1965. When this body style was discontinued, Thunderbird produced no more convertibles.

Any Thunderbird convertible is in demand, as they're fun cars to own and drive. The 1955–57 "Earlybirds" are the most wanted models, with 1958 through 1960 models being least desirable.

WILLYS was sorely ailing when World War II broke out, and the company wisely decided to cash in on the popularity of the famous Jeep. A fancy little Jeepster was offered from 1948 through 1952. Both four- and six-cylinder engines were available, though the bodies were identical. These were open cars in every sense of the word, with manually-operated tops and side curtains. Step plates, reminiscent of rumble seats, were mounted for access to the rear seat.

These sporty little cars proved to be tough as well as fun to drive. They would hold four people, and gave sprightly performance. But low production kept prices high, and not enough were sold to make continuing production profitable. Since they were only produced in small quantities for four years, there aren't many still around. Willys didn't offer a convertible in the Aero line they introduced in 1952. If you can locate a restorable Jeepster at a reasonable price, you'll be lucky indeed.

So you see, the choice is yours. During the post-World War II years convertibles were produced to fit every purse and purpose.

Hard-to-find Willys Jeepster, somewhat spartan in creature comforts, are easy to repair, give excellent service and are fun to drive.

Mechanically these were all good cars, with a tremendous variety of power plants available, from the tiny Crosley four-cylinder engine, to the Lincoln V-12, Chrysler's Hemi-head V-8, and the V-8s offered by Ford and General Motors. Though six-cylinder engines lost some of their popularity until the compact cars appeared in the early 1960s, a wide choice of sixes was offered. Hudson's Hornet with "Twin H power" tops the list for brute power, and the flathead sixes of Pontiac, Ford, Chrysler Corporation, Nash and Studebaker were all dependable and economical. Later the overhead-valve sixes offered by all the manufacturers gave extra power at lighter weight. Chevrolet's air-cooled Corvair engine, a horizontally-opposed six cylinder, gave an excellent power-to-weight ratio. The F-Head engine of the Willy's Jeepster produced a lot of power for a four-cylinder engine.

Many of these convertibles are still around, just waiting for someone to restore them. Like any other group of cars, some are more desirable than others. These will command a higher price when you buy them, but will also demand a higher price when and if you decide to sell. Like any other product, you pay for quality. However, there are convertibles of the post-World War II era available today for as little as $100. These are cars that can be restored to many times this value by work that you can largely do yourself.

Ill-fated Chevrolet Corvair has redeemed itself and is now a popular car to restore. Dependable rear-mounted, air-cooled engine gives these small cars plenty of zip along with good gas mileage.

In the thirty-year span from 1946 to April 1976, when the last U.S.-produced convertible rolled off Cadillac's assembly line, certain convertibles stand out as exceptional cars. These are best buys as investments, for ease of restoration and for driving fun. All convertibles, of course.

1954 BUICK SKYLARK. Low production model with exciting performance, striking styling and some years-ahead features.

1957 CADILLAC ELDORADO BIARRITZ. Limited production car of the highest quality, with many advanced features.

1969 CHEVROLET CORVAIR. Well-styled small car, long rid of any design or mechanical deficiencies. Lively, comfortable and economical. Scarcity increases its value.

1953–55 CHEVROLET CORVETTE. Sheer driving fun in a delightful small car. Uncomplicated, easy to work on. Fiberglass body and other advanced styling features.

1946–50 CHRYSLER TOWN AND COUNTRY. Distinctive wood-trimmed body with luxurious, high-quality interiors. Low production model, now scarce; a real collector's item.

1957 CHRYSLER 300C. Brute performance in a sleek, stylish package. Combines the best traits of a personal car, a sports car and family car. Excellent quality inside and out.

1958–60 EDSEL CITATION. Unique styling and scarcity makes them hard to find but worth the search.

1946–47 FORD SPORTSMAN. Wood-trimmed bodies lift them out of the ordinary, giving them extra value.

1949–54 HUDSON, COMMODORE or HORNET. Excellent road cars. Choose the HORNET for performance, the COMMODORE for luxurious interior detailing. Already scarce.

1964 IMPERIAL CROWN. Size and luxurious interior, plus power and speed, guarantee its value.

KAISER-FRAZER. Both the MANHATTAN and the VIRGINIAN, low production four-door models, will continue to increase in value.

1946–48 LINCOLN CONTINENTAL. The "Queen of the Classics" will continue to increase in value as remaining cars decrease in number.

1946–48 LINCOLN. Very few convertibles produced; overshadowed by the Continental. Well built, stylish and very scarce.

1961–68 LINCOLN CONTINENTAL. America's last four-door convertible. Clean, sophisticated styling. These large cars are beautifully built of top-quality materials. They've long since reached their lowest price.

1946–47 MERCURY SPORTSMAN. Unique wood-trimmed body gives this car increasing value. Very scarce.

1957 OLDSMOBILE GOLDEN ROCKET. Combines high style and high performance, guaranteeing an eager market.

1953 PACKARD CARIBBEAN. High-styled, high-quality car produced in limited quantities, representing the last big push by Packard to compete with Cadillac and Lincoln.

A real collector's item, Buick Skylark grew out of a limited-production dream car. Fine leather upholstery, chrome wire wheels and other goodies were standard equipment.

Minor dents, dings and scratches don't detract from desirability of the solidly built 1964 Oldsmobile 98. Its design has remained attractive, making these cars attractive investments.

1948–50 PACKARD CUSTOM 8. Unexcelled quality of these big cars gives the restorer an opportunity to understand Packard's leadership during the "classic years."

1947–49 STUDEBAKER COMMANDER. Style leaders for their day. These well-built cars are increasing in value because of scarcity.

1955–57 THUNDERBIRD. Stylish and compact, with excellent handling. These favorites are worth searching for; prices will continue to increase as supply decreases.

Many other post-World War II convertibles are fun to restore and drive, though not as exciting, glamorous or unique as the aforementioned cars. These might be considered second choice if the competition to buy the favorites is too stiff for your pocketbook. All are cars you'll enjoy, and should be able to buy for considerably less than the cars in greater demand.

BUICK. Look for the Electra 225's of 1964–65. Though these big cars still carry a fair price tag, they'll only go up more in price in the next few years. They offer about as much luxury as you'll want. The Buick Roadmasters of 1955–57 seem to have been overlooked; they are a lot of car for little money. In the small Buick line, the Special Skylarks (nothing like previous Skylarks) of 1963 and 1964 are recommended as well-finished, attractive, compact convertibles.

CADILLAC. The Series 62 of 1949, a large car well made of high-quality materials, will give excellent service. The 1963 and 1964 DeVille convertibles seem to have been bypassed by restorers, and are really among Cadillac's best cars. Long and low, their styling hasn't become dated as some of the more faddish models. These convertibles are cars you'll enjoy driving.

CHEVROLET. The 1955–57 Bel Air convertibles are excellent performers and are roomy without being overly large. Easy to restore, you'll enjoy the restoration, as well as the knowledge that your car is appreciating in value each month you own it. Still plentiful.

CHRYSLER. The 1955 New Yorker stands out among Chrysler-built cars because of its good looks. The solid, well-made car was sold in sufficient quantities and is not yet scarce. You'll like the feel and performance of these large cars, which are not difficult to restore.

COMET. Though very similar to the Falcon, fewer were produced. The Caliente convertibles of 1963–65 should be a good investment, as well as a nice small car to own.

CROSLEY. These tiny cars command a surprisingly high price because of their rarity. If you can locate a convertible that's not overly priced, it'll be a good buy because of the very few now extant.

DESOTO. Never a large producer of convertibles. The 1957 Fireflite Adventurer offered unusual styling surprises and many

Bolt-on chrome trim decorates this Buick mid-size convertible. Dual headlights nestle in recesses on each side of the grille. Snug-fitting power-operated top lowers into well, giving a sporty appearance.

Restored in every respect except a new top, this Chevrolet will give many miles of pleasurable driving and will continue to increase in value.

Size and quality have kept Cadillac convertibles favorites of restorers who want to see their investment increase in value. They're worth acquiring if priced within reason.

creature comforts. The DeSoto of 1961—the last year of production—is somewhat garish in design but will increase in value because of its rarity.

DODGE. Wayfarer Roadsters of 1949–51 were produced in small quantities so should become good candidates for restoration. The larger, fancier Custom Royal Lancers of 1955 and 1956 have been overlooked by many; they offer a lot of car for the money. The 1963 Dart GT is the most desirable of Dodge's small convertibles.

EDSEL. The Ranger convertibles of any year show a definite resemblance to Fords, but because of their rarity are good buys.

FORD. The 1957–59 Skyliner retractable hardtop convertibles are in demand because of their unique folding steel roof. Really scarce, they appear occasionally, and should continue to increase in value. The 1960 Sunliner, with its graceful styling and curves, offers the restorer an excellent opportunity to realize a profit on his investment.

HUDSON. Because of their rarity, the 1946 and 1947 Commodore convertibles are desirable models.

LINCOLN. The 1952–55 Capri convertibles are good-looking cars that are excellent performers. Quality is evident in their

Dodge put a lot of style and performance into the Coronet convertible. Surprisingly roomy and easy to handle, Dodges are popular convertibles usually inexpensive to restore.

Large Mercury Marquis convertible shows signs of poor color matching on front fender, indicating collision repairs. Check frame and suspension on cars that show obvious repair signs.

Mustang styling has remained popular. Small and lithe, the convertibles are among the easiest cars to restore. There is no problem obtaining replacement parts.

finishing and detailing. The large 1958–60 Continental Mark III convertibles are unique in styling and quite scarce. They'll give the restorer a fine car to drive, and a good investment.

MERCURY. Look for the 1965 and 1966 Park Lanes. These are big cars, nicely styled, and offer a large amount of luxury at a reasonable price.

METROPOLITAN. These sub-compacts, Nash cars with an Austin engine, give sprightly performance and amazing economy of operation. The few that bore the Hudson badge are the more rare.

MUSTANG. The 1965 and 1966 models, before they grew into larger cars and their distinctive styling was corrupted, offer a lot in a small car. They sold well when new, so there are still plenty around. They'll increase in value faster than other compacts of the same year. The 1973 has value because it is the last Mustang convertible.

NASH. The Ramblers of 1950–55 are worth restoring because of their unique fixed window framing. The 1955 Hudson Rambler is very rare. The perky styling of 1961–63 Rambler Americans make them models that will appreciate considerably. The 1967 Ambassador and the 1968 AMC Rebel are notable as the last Nash convertibles.

OLDSMOBILE. The Starfire of 1961 has somehow been overlooked. This is a high-styled model with excellent handling qualities—a nice car to own. The 1964 Olds F-85 Cutlass is the most desirable of the small Oldsmobiles.

PACKARD. The 1953 Mayfair packs Packard's largest Straight

Outside spare on Nash Metropolitan allowed extra luggage space. These little cars are well made and handle nicely. They're quite easy to repair, though parts may be difficult to locate.

Olds Cutlass convertible is a solid, well-performing car, bigger than it looks. Oldsmobiles are popular with restorers because of quality construction and easy-to-obtain replacements.

Eight engine in a well-designed, nicely finished body. Real Packard in every sense, bound to appreciate in value.

PLYMOUTH. The 1963 and 1964 Fury convertibles offer the most of any of Plymouth's full-size cars. Free of earlier styling excesses, they're good-looking, good-handling cars. The 1965

Valiant Signet stands out among Plymouth's compacts as the most desirable model.

PONTIAC. The 1949 Streamliner is a good buy if you can still locate one. The 1953 Star Chief is a lot of car that should increase in value substantially in the years ahead. Pontiac's 1965 Tempest GTO appears to be the compact Pontiac that will find the most favor as time passes.

STUDEBAKER. The 1950–51 Commanders now have considerable value—because of the front-end styling that hurt their sales when new. Value will increase as the remaining few enjoy their rarity.

THUNDERBIRD. Often overlooked in resumes of T-bird popularity, the 1961–63 convertibles are probably a best buy. They're still around, and in surprisingly good condition for cars their age. The graceful curved design will gain popularity as time passes.

WILLYS. Jeepsters of 1948–52 will continue to increase in value as their numbers diminish. You may have trouble locating one, for they sell about as soon as they're offered for sale.

The convertibles listed as "outstanding" for their time, and those "second choices" listed by makes, are by no means the only post-World War II convertibles worth buying. Because convertibles are no longer being produced, all post-World War II models that are kept in good condition, or are in tip-top shape, will appreciate in value, giving their owner a tidy increase when and if the car is sold. If you don't pay too much as compared with other models of the same year, you can't go wrong with any post-World War II convertible.

Unless there is but one particular make, model and year convertible you've just got to have, it's wise to leave yourself some leeway when searching for your car. Decide about how much you want to pay, then look for cars in that price range. Compare the prices of other body styles of the same make and year car, to get an idea of what a given model may be worth. Also compare prices from dealer to dealer, and prices for models you'd like that are advertised in national car magazines. These facts will give you some protection against going overboard when you spot the convertible you want. Decide which general classification of cars you'd

Massive taillights, chrome fender-top molding, and dummy side exhaust ports all contribute to popularity of the third-series Thunderbirds, also known as "Curveybirds," of 1961 thru 1963.

Early T-birds weren't stressed sufficiently to do much trailer pulling. When you look at a car with a trailer hitch, be sure to check its frame for extra bracing, and also check the springs and shocks.

Last of the "Curveybirds," 1963 Thunderbirds have been overlooked in years past but are now recognized for their clean styling. Good cars to restore, their value will increase rapidly.

like: luxury cars, high-performance cars, personal cars, compacts, etc. Within these classifications you'll find several makes from which to choose, making the final acquisition much easier.

As you decide upon these general classifications, keep in mind that generally the larger and more expensive the car originally, the more complex it will be to restore. However, because of extra quality built into more expensive cars, they may not require as much restoration as lower priced models.

The high-performance cars will have much more complex engines and drive trains and, because of their very nature, may have been driven much harder. They may require more mechanical restoration than some other convertibles. Few people bought Chrysler 300's or Corvettes who didn't enjoy the performance these machines provided.

The inexpensive cars obviously provided much less in every detail than the more expensive models. You'll find evidences of this throughout the car—mechanically, as well as in interior appointments. More restoration may be necessary. But to offset this, parts are usually more readily available and less expensive.

If you decide you want a large, luxurious convertible, choose from Cadillacs, Chryslers, Lincolns and Packards. These were the best American manufacturers produced. You'll find a variety of styles and design features. Cadillacs and Packards were a bit more "dressy" than the others. Lincolns were sleek and sophisticated. Chrysler Imperials were more clumsy, with styling gimmicks that quickly dated them. All of these large convertibles had ample power, were well engineered and nicely finished. Leather upholstery was common, and these cars usually had about every automatic device offered.

One step down in quality, though about the same size, were the large Buick Electras, Chrysler New Yorkers, the standard Lincolns, Olds 98's, Packard Clippers and the 200 Series, Hudson Commodores and others. These are all able performers, stylish and comfortable. They offer the restorer a car that will give excellent service and will win the admiring glances of car buffs.

Another group of convertibles that may be only slightly smaller, and less powerful and less luxurious, includes the Buick Super, Chrysler Newport, DeSoto, Hudson Super and Hornet, Edsel, Kaiser-Frazer, Mercury, Olds 88's, Pontiacs and eight-cylinder Studebakers. These cars handle well, were generally well designed, and offer relatively easy restorations.

Priced just above Ford, Chevrolet and Plymouth were the Dodge, six-cylinder Pontiacs, Nash Ambassador, Ford-based Mercury, Ramblers and the six-cylinder Studebakers. These cars weren't overly exciting when new, so they can usually be picked up at a surprisingly low price compared with the cost of other cars of the same year.

There is a whole field of compacts: Buick's Special, Chevrolet Chevelle and Nova, Comet, Dodge Lancer, Falcon, Lark, Olds F-85, Pontiac Tempest, Rambler and Valiant. These are small cars, but they have adequate room and power. Many of them share the same body stampings, making replacement body parts quite easy to find at affordable prices.

Chevrolet, Ford and Plymouth commonly offered two sizes and price ranges most model years. There was one model usually more deluxe than the other. These cars give ample performance and are well worth the time and money it takes to restore them. There's always a ready market for a good Chevrolet, Ford or Plymouth convertible.

A group first promoted as "personal cars" includes the Chrysler 300, Corvette and Thunderbird. Buick's Riviera was designed to compete in this group. These cars soon outgrew this classification and became high-performance cars. They offer almost sports car handling plus high styling, and fairly high prices. They're apt to be rather complicated mechanically, and more expensive to restore.

If you shop around you can pick up a restorable post-World War II convertible for as low as $100, possibly even less. Obviously a car selling for such a price will need complete restoration. The lower the price, the more work required to make a satisfactory restoration. However, if that's all you want to pay, you can start the fun of restoring a convertible, and stretch other costs over the restoration period. The amount the car will finally cost depends upon the car's condition and your ability to do a lot of the work yourself.

3

Let the Buyer Beware

T ake the time necessary to examine carefully the cars that interest you. If you have a friend who is knowledgeable about mechanical parts, don't hesitate to ask for advice. A test drive will help determine the condition of the engine, transmission, steering and brakes. Lift the car on a service-station grease rack to look for damage that may not be visible from above.

Pay particular attention to weld marks on the frame, indicating wreck repairs. Look for transmission and power-steering unit leaks. Check sagging springs and broken shock absorbers. If the car has towed a trailer, look for rear spring and shock absorber wear. Also listen for differential whine when driving. Check uneven tire wear indicating bent wheels or poor alignment. Look for rust on the floor, as well as rusted-through rocker panels. Examine the muffler and exhaust pipe.

Pick the car in the best mechanical condition. Normally mechanical repairs will cost more than body repairs, so keep that in

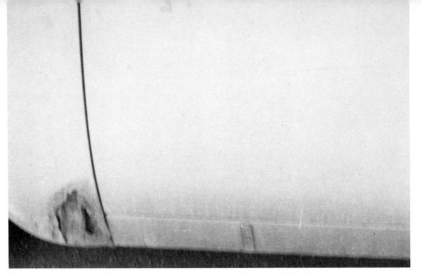

Dirt that collected between support and fender panel held moisture, causing rust-through. Plan on spending about two hours cutting out old metal and welding in a new piece. Schedule another hour for finishing.

mind as you look. A convertible with a rough body, poor upholstery and a shredded top, but in sound mechanical condition, will be less expensive to restore than a car with top and upholstery in average condition that needs a lot of work on the motor, transmission, suspension system, brakes, etc. So don't be turned off by rough appearance if the mechanical condition is good.

Overall mechanical condition depends less upon the mileage indicated on the odometer than the care and maintenance the car has received. A well-maintained, high-mileage car is usually a better buy than a car with lower mileage that has been abused and neglected.

There are some conditions you should check very carefully as you look for a convertible to restore. The time and effort devoted to these checks will be well worth the while.

Rust and damage from moisture are the biggest enemies of old cars. This is especially true of convertibles. Damage and wear to the fabric top can allow water to leak into body panels and onto upholstery. Interior hardware often will be rusted and inoperative.

Unfortunately, many of the style trends that developed in the 1950s and 1960s invited the car's eventual deterioration by rust. Areas around headlights, rocker panels and plated trim parts all retained dirt and moisture, inviting rust. This seems particularly evident on some Ramblers and Studebakers, as well as on 1957 and 1958 Fords, and Chrysler and General Motors compacts.

Rust-through ahead of fender and behind rocker panel will require three or four hours to repair. You can either weld in new metal or make a fiberglass patch, since area is not structural.

Another design deficiency seems to have been failure to provide adequate drainage for moisture that seeped into body panels, doors and cowl sections.

Often cars were left standing outdoors with the top down or the rear curtain open, allowing the sun to fade and practically scorch upholstery. Leaves and other debris drifted into the car, and rain may have soaked everything. Over an extended period, moisture could accumulate in seldom-cleaned areas, causing rusted metal and decayed fabrics.

Decaying upholstery fabrics exposed seat frames and springs to moisture, causing the formation of rust. Rotting carpets let water soak into underlying padding, in turn rusting out sections of the floor.

Front fender on this Camaro can be hammered into basic shape with bumping hammer, then finished with dinging hammer and hand dolly. This will be half a day's work for the beginner, not counting finishing.

An inexpensive fiberglass patch will satisfactorily repair rust-damaged area on this Chevrolet. Allow a couple of hours for the repair, and probably two hours more for sanding, priming and painting.

As drain holes in the bottoms of doors and body panels became clogged, retained water caused rust inside these panels and decay in upholstery. Often seat-adjustment mechanisms, window regulators and the top lowering/raising mechanisms fail to work easily or properly because of rust damage.

Owners who traded cars every year or two often attended only to the car's basic mechanical condition and didn't bother with the top or any preventive maintenance for the body. You'll spot these omissions as you examine the car.

Some dealers selling used convertibles concentrate on cosmetic detailing only. They cover rusted body panels and fenders with a flashy paint job over improperly repaired panels. This allows rust to spread undetected until serious rust damage occurs. When buying your convertible for restoration, determine the extent of rust

It's not unusual to find the interior of a convertible in this condition after having been left standing for a year or so with the top lowered. Reupholstering will cure the problem.

damage to the body, and the amount of rot and decay to the top, seats, carpets and upholstery panels.

Check the following components carefully, and record your findings on Part I of Checklist A at the back of this book. Be honest with yourself, and make an accurate report. The only one you'll be fooling will be yourself.

EXTERIOR

FENDERS: Examine one fender at a time. Remember that on many convertibles of the late 1950s and the 1960s the rear fender actually starts at the rear of the front door. On others there is a discernible rear fender. Look for dents and creases in the metal. Check where each fender joins the body or other panels. Look for obvious rust in seams. Check very carefully for paint blisters, which indicate below-the-surface rust. Check for rust around the headlights, taillights, turn signals, or other plated parts attached to the fenders. If there is a chrome rub strip along the side of the car, or other bright metal moldings, check for rust around these. Look for rust or paint blisters where the bumper splash aprons, grilles and other accessories are mounted. Make these checks fender by fender. Be thorough, and record your findings in the proper spaces on Checklist A.

Gouges and dents along the side of this Dodge are neither serious nor expensive to repair. Door dent can be pushed out from the inside. A beginner should allow a day for this type of job.

Creases on front fender of this Chrysler should pull out. Drill holes about one inch apart along crease, then use dent hook pullers. Fill area with epoxy filler, using several thin coats.

Though not expensive to repair, allow the better part of a day to repair damage to this Chevrolet's fender and bent bumper. Use solvent to loosen bumper bolts. An epoxy filler will smooth the fender.

ROCKER PANELS: These bottom-most side pieces of body metal usually take a beating from scrapes against curbs, rocks thrown up by the wheels, and large objects over which the car may have been driven. On some models the rocker panel extends from the front wheel arch to the rear wheel arch, and may be three or four inches in height. On others, a rocker panel was fitted only under the doors, with the fenders extending to the bottom of the body. Look for dents, creases, rusted metal, rust holes, and weakened metal under paint blisters. You may find a plated trim piece along the rocker panel, which often hides rust; check around the edges of any plated trim piece on the rub strip. You'll find a place to record your findings on Checklist A.

It's better to leave fender on car when repairing this type of damage. A jack stand will hold car in solid, safe position when wheel is removed. Use bumper hammer first, then dinging hammer.

Small piece inserted on rocker panel below door on this 1949 Ford exemplifies a poorly made repair. Check carefully along rest of rocker panel area to determine extent of damage.

COWL SECTION: These panels, the front section of the car's body, vary greatly in size and style. The cowl is the section against which the hood is hinged, or to which it closes if it's hinged at the grille. Depending upon the designer's idea, the cowl may be hidden on cars on which the front fender is another body panel, with only a cutout for the front wheel. In these cases, common from the 1960s on, the cowl panel is really a bulkhead, the front of which is the firewall. You'll have to raise the hood to look in the space between the side portion of the cowl and the inside of the fender panels. Many times water draining from the roof and windshield ran down between these panels and was trapped, causing rust.

On cars of the 1940s and 1950s (with the exception of slab-sided cars) there was a separate and recognizable cowl panel, and each side can be checked carefully. Look for rust around the bottoms, as well as around top- or side-mounted cowl ventilators.

The cowl section, whether visible or not, is most important on convertible bodies as it must support the doors (unless they're hinged at the back) and windshield without the additional bracing and strength the metal roof provides on hardtops. Look for rust around the windshield frame, paint blisters around any seams, as well as evidence of improperly repaired collision damage. Open the front doors and check for rust where the door hinges attach. Check very carefully for rust and paint blisters at the bottom of

Rust around wheel arches should be cleaned out, then repaired with a fiberglass patch or epoxy filler. Cement will hold hanging letter in place. Jobs like these don't cost much and make a great improvement.

Determine extent of damage along seams in body panels and wheel cutouts. Plated trim must be removed and the rust scraped clean. Either new metal or a fiberglass patch will correct the problem.

each door pillar, which is the rear portion of the cowl. List your findings on Checklist A.

DOORS: Check each door separately. See if each is properly aligned to open easily and close solidly. On the outside, any stripes or moldings on the doors should line up with the corresponding stripe or molding on adjoining panels. Misaligned doors may indicate a midsection repair that has been improperly done. Check where each hinge is attached to the door to be sure there is no rust in these areas. The support to which the door closes should also be free from rust and should not show signs of faulty collision repairs. Check the bottoms of the doors, plus the bottom sills of the door openings. Many times the drain openings on doors will become clogged, allowing water to rust the inside of the doors. There may be bright metal sill plates, but rust often forms around and under these plates. Be sure to scrape any paint blisters to see the extent of damage to underlying metal. By looking at each door from an oblique angle you may see ripples or other evidence of patching with body filler. This indicates less-than-perfect repair, which calls for new metal or fiberglass and repainting.

Rotted or decayed upholstery panels on the door may indicate serious rust-through on the inner door panels caused by moisture trapped inside the door. Record your findings door by door on Checklist A.

BODY PANELS: Light surface rust and minor dings and dents aren't serious but will require repair and touch-up. Hardly a car has been parked in a supermarket parking lot that hasn't received some marks from other cars. These are unimportant to the overall sound condition of the car but must be reckoned with in a restoration project. Check the lower portion of each panel to detect paint

To stop rust spreading from scrapes along the side, sand carefully and use epoxy filler to smooth the area. Replacement side strip from a two-door sedan will fit a Nova convertible.

Light rust and missing pieces of molding give this Chevrolet a shabby appearance and detract from its value. A few hours and some small pieces of molding will do wonders.

Unless scrapes on Buick door are repaired, rust will spread through outer skin. When you find molding strips that don't line up, check hinge before changing placement of molding.

blisters and rust-through. Body putty and plastic filler may indicate incomplete and improper repairs to collision damage. Check the edges of each panel, and any seams in a panel. Check where the panel meets the upright door supports, looking for obvious rust, paint blisters, and creases that may have been filled with body putty rather than being properly straightened.

If the car you're considering has separate rear fenders, check the body metal where the fender is attached. In some cases there may be raised body molding accenting and stiffening this joint. It should be free of rusted spots or rust-through. Make a thorough check where the bottom front edge of the rear fender meets the body. This spot sometimes attracts rust because inadequate provision was made in the car's design for draining moisture that collects here. On some cars a rubber or plated piece may be attached to the bottom leading edge of the rear fender. The space between this and the adjoining body panel often holds dirt and moisture, causing rust.

On cars where the rear fender is really a long body panel with a cutout for the wheel, check the area ahead and behind the wheel arch. Dirt thrown up by the tires often collects in these areas, holding moisture and causing rust-through.

Stand a few feet away from each panel and view it from an angle. Previously made repairs will show up quickly, unless they've been expertly done. Look for pitting around plated trim parts and around the area where the roof joins the body. List all damage you spot on each panel on Checklist A.

To keep rust on wheel cutout from spreading, clean both sides of metal, then fill with epoxy filler. Undercoat inside of fender and repaint outside area. Regularly cleaning inside fenders prevents rust.

Check to see if door is sprung when you notice a vertical crease close to the hinge area. If you don't want to remove upholstery panel to push out the metal, use pull hooks and epoxy filler.

DECK LID: Check alignment of the lid all around the opening. The distance between the body and deck lid should be the same on each side. Check the hinges and hinge mountings. On cars where the hinges were externally mounted, they should be complete and free from pitting or rust. Look for rust damage at the bottom of the lid, as this area is prone to rust on many cars. Check for rust and scale around lights, license plate brackets, lid handle and lock, and other plated parts attached to the deck lid. Check the rubber weather stripping around the deck opening. It should be complete and free from tears that could cause leakage into the rear deck, with resulting rust and decay to carpeting. Check the operation of the lock and handle, as well as the mechanism to hold the lid open. In some cars this may be a rod; on others the deck hinges are spring loaded to hold the lid open. List all your findings on Checklist A.

PANEL BELOW DECK LID: On some cars this may be concealed when the lid is closed; on others it may extend a few inches below the lid to the bottom of the body. If the car was involved in a rear-end collision and repairs didn't properly mate the lid and the panel below the lid, there's the risk of water leaking into the compartment and finding some spot to rust. Check where this panel joins the rear fenders or fender body panels. If there is a splash

Remove bumper face bar to expose rust-through in panel below deck lid. Scrape out all rust, then either weld in new metal or use epoxy filler. When properly finished, repair won't show.

Rust-through at bottotm of wheel well must be cut out and a new well formed and welded in place. If restorer isn't hooked on authenticity, flat metal floor can be welded in to replace well.

apron between the bumper and the rear deck, there should be no rust or pitting along the seam. In some cars this narrow panel is decorated with a plated strip, while in others lights or license plate brackets are mounted on it. Check around anything that is mounted to this panel, looking for rust, scale or paint blisters. Though the area you're checking in this instance isn't very large, it is very important to the car's structural integrity and should be checked carefully. Record your appraisal of this panel on Checklist A.

HOOD: You can usually see at a glance all you may think you need to know about the hood. Rust or damaged areas should be spotted quickly. However, don't let it go at that. Check to see if the hood is properly aligned. The distance between the edges of the hood panel and the fender or fender panel should be equidistant. If they're not, the hood is out of alignment and you should determine why. This may be the result of a front-end collision that has knocked the car out of alignment. Check where the hood is attached to the hinges, looking for crimped metal on any inner hood bracing as well as signs of repair to the hood hinges. The hood should shut firmly at the grille (or at the cowl if front-hinged), and the panel shouldn't flutter when the car is moving. It should also close as tightly on one side as on the other, with neither edge projecting above the adjoining body panels. Check for rust and paint blisters around moldings and any attached plated trim parts. If there is an ornament at the front, see if this is complete, firmly attached, and not rusted where it is mounted to the hood. List your findings on Checklist A.

PAINT: You should get a good idea of the condition of the paint as you examine the exterior parts of the car. As previously mentioned, small scratches and marks that come from everyday driving experiences aren't serious and shouldn't detract from your decision on the car. But be alert for large touch-up spots and panels that have been repainted. Modern repair shops can do an excellent job of repairing, and once a damaged car has been repaired properly, you needn't be wary of buying it. It's the hastily half-repaired cars you should check extra carefully. Large areas of paint that don't match the rest of the car are evidence of a poor repair job. Areas that show patched places beneath the paint haven't been feathered properly, indicating a poor repair was made.

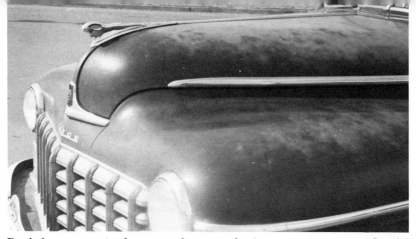

Don't let worn paint keep you from purchasing a car you want. Careful sanding, priming, second sanding and paint will make this Dodge look like new. Either remove or mask chrome.

Worn paint on door, or any panel, can be sanded, primed and re-painted. It's more satisfactory to refinish entire panel rather than try area touch-ups. Usually there is no trouble matching paint.

If you stand a few feet away from the car and view it at an angle, large uneven or rippled areas indicate poor repairs.

Many cars, especially old ones, may have been repainted once or twice. This doesn't indicate collision repair, and shouldn't make you suspect serious damage. You can easily check on the quality of a repaint job by looking at the areas around attached chrome parts. On a first-class paint job these would have been removed so the new finish could protect the metal underneath. If the part was simply masked off, you can usually see evidences where the masking tape was either improperly applied or a spot was missed. When the car was new, rubber washers between attached plated

Minor scrape on this Impala can be filled with epoxy, and dents at rear of fender panel can be hammered out. The area should be sanded, primed, sanded a second time and painted before new side molding is fitted.

parts and the car were black. On a repaint where the part wasn't removed, this rubber washer will be the color of the car.

Look on the inside of the doors and the door support pillars. These should be the same color as the outside. Any identification plate will not be painted on an original paint job, nor on a first-class repaint job. Stickers from a service station indicating dates and mileage of service should not be painted. If you peel off the sticker, the metal underneath should be the same color as that around it.

The fire wall and the area under the hood panel will be the same color as the outside on an original paint job, or on a first-class re-paint job. If these areas aren't the same color as the outside of the car, you'll know the sort of paint job that was done. The rubber molding around door, deck lid and hood opening should be black or dark-colored rubber, not the color of the car. If you lift the outer edge of one of these rubber moldings, the metal underneath should be the same color as the metal on the outside.

Your real interest in the paint job is to determine damages the car may have received, and the care and extent to which they have been repaired. You may decide you want the car a different color anyway, so you can judge for yourself just how important the present paint is in your plans. Record your findings on Checklist A.

CHROME PLATING: Though this is important only to the appearance of the car, having nothing to do with the way the car

Plan on removing worn weather stripping and cleaning the area thoroughly before painting and replacing strip, which is inexpensive. Check the door latch mechanism for wear.

Door should be removed from Caprice for repair. When upholstery panel is removed, both inner and outer panel can be straightened. Repairs to fender panel should be made before door is replaced.

Don't let damage like this keep you from considering a car. The panel can be pushed out from inside, and small dents hammered out. New molding clips in place. Other minor detailing will be necessary.

Dented bumper parts can either be hammered straight or pressed back in place. Rust spots must be ground bare before being replated. Use solvent on bolts so bumper can be disassembled for repair.

operates, you probably will want the chrome shiny and glistening at some point. Pitting or spots on which the plating has peeled loose indicates a need for eventual replating. Examine the bumpers, grille, headlight and taillight bezels, side moldings, and other bolt-on plated parts. Mark on Checklist A any part you believe below the standard you consider acceptable. If the grille seems to need plating, examine the way it is assembled. Many cars have grilles made up of several sections, and perhaps only portions of the grille will need replating. Also check chrome frames around the windows, and record your findings.

GLASS: Glass is easily replaced in most cases, but an expense that should be considered as you appraise the car. Check the windshield and side windows for cracks, small holes, and discoloration, and record your findings on Checklist A. Remember you can't make an insurance claim on glass that is broken before you buy the car and have it insured.

INTERIOR

FLOORS: Even if the rest of the body shows little or no rust damage, lift the floor mats or carpets and examine the condition of the floors. Also look under the mat in the trunk, and at the bottom of the well that holds the spare wheel. If you find rust in any of these places, scrape a bit with a penknife or screwdriver to see the extent of the rust. The strength of the floors is most important to the overall strength of the body, so don't treat this part of your examination lightly.

If you find moisture in the padding under the carpets, or in the backing of rubber mats, you can be certain there'll be rust damage in time if the source of the leak isn't corrected. List your findings

Serious rust-through on Packard floor requires that the old metal be cut out and new metal welded in place. Because driveshaft tunnel must be shaped, an accomplished welder will probably take six hours.

on Checklist A, Part II, to be considered when you make your overall evaluation of the car.

UNDER SEATS: If you found no rust under the carpets and floor mats you needn't worry about rust under the front seat. However, if you found areas that were rusted through, or large patches of rust on the floor, examine the floor under the seat. To do this you may have to lift out the front seat cushion and turn back the carpet. If you find rusted places on the floor under the seat, examine the spots at which the front seat track is attached to the floor. There will usually be two spots on each side. If your car has bucket seats there will be four tracks with two mountings per track. It's important that seat mountings be firm and secure, as a matter of safety.

If you found rust on the floor of the rear compartment as well as in the luggage space, you'd better have a look at the floor under the rear seat. This often receives water that pours in if the rear curtain isn't closed securely during wet weather. Lift out the rear seat cushion to spot rust that may have formed. It is at the sides of this area, as well as at the back, that the top-operating mechanism

Though fairly well protected against rust damage, look for leaks into interior of car where the top joins the body. The large, late-model Fords will remain popular with high resales.

A bumper shop will use a hydraulic press to remove dent from this Olds bumper. Small panel at front of fender can either be replaced or repaired. The cost of these repairs is low and should be made.

is located, and this should be rust-free. Record any rusted floor areas on Checklist A, Part II.

STRUCTURAL SUPPORTS: These upright portions of the body, ahead and behind the doors and at the back of the area into which the top folds, are very important on convertibles because of the lack of rigid top supports. If the car shows evidence of collision damage, look underneath to see the extent of the damage and the kind of repairs that were made. Modern repair shops can rebuild a damaged car good as new, and evidence of collision repairs properly made shouldn't worry you. If you can have the car put on a hoist, take a good look under it, noting any patches welded in place as well as rusted spots that may not as yet be visible from the outside. You can easily spot torn metal, and this should alert you to the fact the car has been in a collision. If you notice such damages, have the car checked for proper alignment at a shop specializing in these services (you'll find them listed in the yellow pages of you phone book).

Evidence of plastic body fillers on the floor or on any of the door and body supports should warn you of hasty, improper repair. Check for rust or weakened metal where the upright supports join the floor. Weakness here will have to be repaired, so record your findings.

TOP AND TOP BOWS: Torn or fraved top fabric is obvious.

A torn roof, as on this Mustang, allows water to seep inside body, where it'll be trapped by clogged drain holes or dirt, and rust will form. Beginner can easily make a new top.

Look for rotted, weakened or brittle fabric that will tear or split easily. Check for spots in the top material, as well as in the weather stripping above the windows, that may have been pinched by the folding top supports. Look for seams that may have split or torn apart. Examine the padding and webbing for strength. The snaps and closures should be in place and should fasten securely. Check the rear window curtain for discoloration or tears. Work the zipper closure. See if the top boot is still with the car, and check its condition. Examine the rubber moldings and the cloth-covered moldings around windows and door openings.

The roof bows should not be bent and should be firmly attached to the folding support arms. Fastenings on the front bow to the windshield frame should be securely mounted, holding the bow tightly to the windshield frame. Operate the power-top mechanism; it should raise easily and evenly. Record your findings on Checklist A, Part II.

SEATS: Look for splits, tears and worn-through areas on the seat cushions. Check for springs that may be broken and exposed. If there's a folding armrest, check the condition of the upholstery on it, as well as the well into which it folds. Look for cigarette burns. If the seats are upholstered in leather, look for tears in the hides, and for stitching that may have pulled loose. Operate the seat adjustment mechanism and backlocks that hold the folding seat in position. Determine if the entire seat will need reupholstering, or if repairs to certain sections will suffice. Record the findings on Checklist A, Part II.

SIDE UPHOLSTERY: Examine the upholstery on each door and side panel. See if it matches or if a substitute or poor replacement has been installed. Look for wear on upholstery panels around door and window hardware. Look at the armrests to determine their condition. Check the edges of the door and side panels to see if they're torn or scuffed. Make sure the door and window hardware is complete, and that each works properly. Check the scuff pads at the bottom of door and upholstery panels; on some cars this may be pieces of carpeting, on others simulated leather. Look at the kick pads under the dashboard to be sure they're in good condition, not worn. Determine if any soiled spots or marks on the upholstery can be cleaned satisfactorily, or will the material have to be replaced? Some cars had bright metal molding strips on door and upholstery panels. Arc these complete? Are they solidly in place? Check the sun visors to be sure they're complete, including any holding device that may be on the windshield frame. Determine if their appearance suits you. Write your findings in the proper place on Checklist A, Part II.

CARPETS AND FLOOR MATS: Examine the carpets and floor mats, looking for worn-through spots, tears, cigarette burns and any decayed or rotted spots. If the heel pads sewed on the front carpeting are worn through, check the wear on the pedals, as these may indicate more miles than might be shown on the odometer. Determine if the carpet can be cleaned or repaired satisfactorily, or if it must be replaced. There's a place on the checklist for your findings.

DASHBOARD: Is the dashboard complete? Is it in condition that can be made presentable by cleaning? See if the instruments all work, and that all knobs perform their function. Check the glove box. Be sure the inside is solid and complete. If there's a lock for the glove box, see if it operates. If there's a console between the dash and the front seats, check it for condition and completeness, and record your findings.

ACCESSORIES: The convenience and enjoyment of most accessories depends upon their working properly. If the car has an air-conditioner, heater-defroster, radio, tape deck or other accessories, most of which were options, check the operation of each. List your findings on the checklist.

When you've completed your careful check of the exterior and interior of the car, and have recorded your findings on Checklist A, you'll have a good idea of the car's condition. A well-documented list of needed repairs may influence your decision on purchasing the car. If in your opinion too many things need replacement or repair, you'll know you're in for a lot of expense and work, and you'll have to make your own decision if the car is worth this amount to you.

A well-documented list of needed repairs should also help you arrive at a price you want to pay. It should give you good bargaining power with the seller, and may save you many dollars on the final purchase price.

The checklist will be the basis for planning your restoration, figuring priorities and estimating costs. Make it carefully, and use it wisely.

II

RESTORING
YOUR
CONVERTIBLE

4

Claiming Your Prize

Once you've completed the deal and the convertible is yours, take special care getting it to its new home. Remember to check motor vehicle laws and traffic regulations that pertain to towing and driving cars on which the title hasn't been changed to your name.

Take some snapshots of the inside and outside of the car, for they'll make interesting comparisons with snapshots you take during the restoration and when you've completed the job.

With the car safely in your garage, you're ready to review Checklist A and consider Checklist B. The value of B is really in scheduling your time and expenditures so you can make the maximum use of each. Checklist B calls for you to estimate the time it will take to either repair or replace a part, as well as the cost of parts and materials. Be as realistic as you can in making these estimates. Of course, if neither restoration costs nor time are

If you tow home your newly acquired convertible, be sure tow bar is securely fastened. If the car has automatic transmission, the drive shaft must be disconnected at the rear universal.

of particular interest to you, you can skip Checklist B and start working.

To get the most satisfaction out of restoring a car, and to save money also, you should plan on doing most if not all of the restoration yourself. Get cost estimates on any jobs you can't do, such as machine shop work, welding or plating. You can get these costs by dropping in or phoning the various shops listed in your newspaper's classified pages or in the yellow pages. You can get the costs of materials and replacement parts from auto supply stores or catalogs.

Plan to complete all the necessary mechanical repairs before starting body restoration. This is the logical progression so you won't run the risk of scarring your newly painted fender while tuning your motor.

If it appears that the restoration will require considerable time, position the car in your garage so you can work all around it safely and easily. If you remove the wheels, use properly placed jack stands. Be sure the jack stands are built to hold at least half the weight of the car per stand; this will give you a margin of safety. Never leave the car standing on regular jacks, bricks, boxes or pieces of lumber when the wheels are removed.

As you remove parts, mark them with string tags or masking tape so you can identify them later. Felt-tip markers in different colors are handy too. For instance, use red to identify parts on the

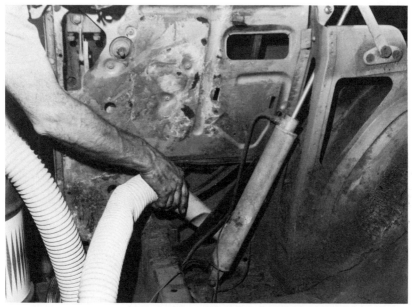

Use a vacuum cleaner to get dirt and other debris from between body panels, under seats and from other crevices. Spray a rust-inhibiting primer for protection.

Badly worn upholstery panels should be removed for reupholstering. Those panels that have metal backing will be held in place by screws. Fiber-backed panels may use screws in addition to clips.

If present carpet isn't good enough to use as a pattern, take measurements and make a pattern. Carpeted kick panels often have a fiber backing anchored with screws and clips.

left side and green for parts on the right side. If you remove the fabric top or worn upholstery panels and carpets, save what you can for patterns. There's no point keeping small bits of the roof or carpet, but be sure you've taken what measurements you may need before discarding them.

If you indicated on Checklist A that some parts are badly rusted or broken, you may find that buying replacements from a wrecking yard or another restorer is to your advantage. Flea markets and swap meets are often a fine source for parts as well as accessories. Some of the benefits of belonging to a car club are the chances that you can locate parts and also get valuable information and helpful hints from other club members.

Remember that many body components such as fenders, doors, deck lids, bumpers, grilles and other trim parts were used on the same makes for two or three model years or more. Manufacturers normally used the same basic body shell for two, three or four years, with only minor trim changes on a year-to-year basis. So you may find just the replacement body parts you need on the same make car a year or two newer or older than yours.

Many of the body stampings for two-door sedans, hardtops and convertibles are the same below the car's belt line. This common practice allows you to pick up some body parts that will fit perfectly from the same make car as yours but a different body style.

Flea markets are an excellent source for parts. You may want to take certain parts with you to be sure replacements match. Often you can swap your excess parts for needed ones.

You probably won't want to buy a parts car, but if you can locate one in a wrecking yard you can often buy all the parts you'll need for a few bucks. Try to anticipate your needs if possible.

You have another source for parts. Look for suitable interchangeable replacement body parts from other cars produced by the same parent company. Most car companies produced two or more makes using the same basic body stampings, as well as some identical mechanical parts. The Comet and Falcon, Cougar and

Mustang, Mercury and Lincoln, as well as Ford and Mercury are examples. The Buick Special, Chevrolet Nova, Olds F-85 and Pontiac Tempest are examples of GM's compacts that are very similar. Some Buick Riviera and Olds Toronado parts are interchangeable, as are some Toronado and Cadillac Eldorado parts. Many full-size General Motors cars shared basic body parts. Chrysler, DeSoto, Dodge and Plymouth all shared many components, as did the AMC-built cars. So by all means, if the findings you recorded on Checklist A indicate replacement parts, look into these look-alike, built-alike cars.

One way to figure the cost of restoration is to take your convertible to a body shop and get an estimate on repairs and repainting. You can also take the car to a trim shop and get the costs of reupholstering or of making and fitting a new top. Indicate that you'd like the estimates broken down as nearly as possible for the various components, as well as for time and labor. These estimates can be used as a guide in figuring your own time for each job. You must

Interior trim items are available from wrecking yards. Many items used in one car will be similar to that used in another make by the same manufacturer. Plated items often clean up easily.

Clips and screws usually attach the upholstery panel to inner door panel. With armrest and hardware removed, upholstery can be taken off. Look for rust along the bottom. Open any plugged drain holes.

realize, however, that the estimates are from professionals who may possess labor-saving tools and techniques not available to you.

The overall condition of each component as listed on Checklist A becomes your guide in determining needed repairs. Any part you indicated as being beyond repair should be replaced.

You may have done enough work on cars to be able to estimate the time and material costs for restoration of the various components. If so, fill in Checklist B and you're on your way.

However, if you're a beginning restorer and have never worked on a car before, you probably won't know how to estimate the time required for the various tasks. This is where the estimates from body shops, auto trim shops, etc. will be helpful. Another way to estimate time requirements is to pick one particular job—say a badly rusted and dented fender—and record the time it takes to repair or replace it.

You may choose to replace the fender rather than trying to repair it. If so, locate and price the replacement. Next, determine how and where the fender is attached to the rest of the car. You can get some tips on this by watching the removal of the replacement fender in a wrecking yard. (When buying replacement parts from wrecking yards, be sure to get all nuts, bolts, washers, springs, etc. that come with the parts.) Determine how many other parts must be removed or disconnected so you can remove the present fender. Consider these questions when estimating time: Can you get at the nuts and bolts as the car now stands, or must you remove a wheel or bumper? Must trim parts be removed? Does any wiring for lights or turn signals have to be removed or disconnected? These and similar questions must be answered so you can estimate the time it will take to remove the old fender and install a new one. You can use the same method for estimating time necessary for replacement of other body parts.

On the other hand, if you decide to repair the fender rather than replace it, estimate the time required to disconnect lights, trim parts and anything that must be removed so you can make necessary repairs. If the fender requires welding, you can phone for time and materials charges at welding shops, though most welders would prefer to see the job before giving a firm quote.

Many bumpers are composed of several parts bolted together. You may need only certain replacement parts for repairs. If they're to be replated, you'll save money by disassembling them yourself.

Many welding shops have mobile units that come out to do the job on site. In these cases a mileage charge is usually added.

A phone call or visit to an automotive supply house can get you prices on fillers, primers, sandpaper and other materials you'll need to repair a fender or other body panels.

The time required for shaping the fender, pounding out dents, filing, sanding, filling and priming, etc. must be a rough estimate on your first job. As you learn your capabilities, estimates on other tasks should become more realistic. This experience will allow you to complete Checklist B, if you choose to use it, with a good deal of accuracy.

If you aren't particularly interested in the amount of time each separate job will take and prefer just to work along at your leisure, skip the "time" portion of the estimate and only fill in the portion that pertains to expenses. You can keep track of your time and write it in the proper place after you've completed each job. One reason for keeping track of the time in the past tense is so you'll have a better idea of time requirements should you decide to restore another car. Another reason for keeping track of your time is to figure overall investment in the car should you decide to sell it.

When you've completed the cost and time estimates you have a good idea of what's ahead of you. Knowing the approximate cost of materials, you'll be able to plan your restoration project to fit any budget you may have set up for the project. You'll also be able to plan restoration for maximum efficiency at minimum time and expense. If you plan to rent tools or equipment, Checklist B will be helpful in planning to rent items only as you need them.

To have the best paint job without any touch-ups, paint your car as the last project in its restoration. Plan the jobs that need to be done in a logical manner. For instance, if you remove the running boards for repair or recovering, also remove the running board brackets so you don't bump your shins every time you go by. If the bumpers and other trim parts will need plating, and if your budget allows, remove them and get them to the plater's so they'll be out of your way as you work on something else. You may get a lower price by having all or most of the plating done at one time.

You can often avoid making new backing panels by replacing only the rotted portion. When the new upholstery is in place the repair won't show. When making new panels, cut control holes first.

Some parts, such as wire wheels, bumper arms and gas tank aprons, may be too rusted or pitted for you to sand them to an acceptable condition. In these cases consider the services of a sandblasting firm or a metal stripper. For only a few dollars these outfits can clean scale and rust off in a hurry. You may want to have these services performed while you're working on other parts. Once parts are sandblasted or stripped, wash them to remove any sand particles or chemical residue. They should be sprayed with a primer coat to prevent rust from forming before you get around to using them.

The way you plan your work will make a lot of difference in the ease and efficiency of restoration. Generally, you'll find it's better to first complete the main body work, such as structural repairs. Door, floors, door framings and supports, and cowl sections are all considered structural components of the body. To repair these you'll usually have to remove upholstery panels or floor coverings. You may have to remove the seat frames and supports. Directions for these jobs follow in Chapter V. Any weakness in upright supports, cowl or floor should be repaired before you start on fenders, doors, body panels or outside components.

For best results, plan to do the body work from the inside first. This may require some dismantling of interior components to allow working room.

Dents in fenders and panels can be pounded out and metal sprung back in place, ready for grinding, filing, sanding, filling and priming. Each of these steps will be covered in detail in later chapters. Don't underestimate the amount of body work you can do yourself using simple, easy-to-acquire tools. If there are rusted-through sections on floors, doors and body panels, you can probably cut out the rusted metal with a saber saw or metal shears. If not, a welding shop can cut it out for you. With the rusted-through metal removed, you may see gaping holes in floors, doors and body panels that make you wonder if you bit off more than you can chew. Don't come unglued at this point; a few hours work and replacement metal will change the looks completely.

If you're watching expenses closely and can only budget a limited number of outside repair expenses at a time, you may want to have only certain portions of the replacement metal welded in place on one call, planning to have the remainder done at another time. If you must make this decision, consider the mileage charge most mobile welding shops make for this service. You may save money by removing doors, certain style fenders and other parts that need welding and taking them to the welding shop to have necessary repairs made.

Rotted upholstery and rusted springs require that seat be removed for repair and reupholstery. Since there's nothing left to use as a pattern, take measurements after repairing spring frames.

Disassemble parts that need to be repaired at a workbench or location other than on the car. If necessary, make a simple diagram of how the part is disassembled so you'll have no trouble putting things back together.

When you've completed body repairs, start on the fenders. Usually these can be repaired satisfactorily on the car. Occasionally it will be easier to remove the fender from the car, make the necessary repairs, then remount it. Work on one fender at a time until you have all four repaired. Directions on how to make body and fender repairs are covered in Chapter V.

If upholstery panels and seats need repairing or reupholstering, plan on doing these jobs at a workbench or other fairly large area. Save all the hardware you remove from doors and panels, and store them in a container marked to show just what parts they are. Note how things come apart so you can reassemble them in reverse order. A simple sketch may help, or a snapshot of the assembled component. Keep as many pieces of upholstery as necessary for patterns. Note any trim that runs from panel to panel, and take the necessary measurements so you can make these panels line up correctly on their replacements. Note too, on cars that have two-tone upholstery or use two types or patterns of upholstery material, how the graining or patterns run, as well as how these areas on doors and side panels line up with corresponding areas on seat cushions.

Directions on upholstery repairs and replacements for doors, side panels and seat cushions are covered in detail in Chapter VI.

Use Checklist B wisely and you'll find your restoration will progress easier, and in the long run you'll save both time and money.

5

Rust Is Out!

If you're a beginning restorer, a general knowledge of auto body construction will be helpful in your restoration. There are two types of body construction used in U.S.-made cars. The first is the unitized body-frame method, in which body parts are welded together, with each panel bracing another and the whole unit providing the necessary strength and rigidity. Stub frames provide for the engine, power train and suspension system attachments. Not many convertible bodies were made this way, because of the lack of rigid top panels. Lincoln Continentals and some Hudsons are examples of this type of body construction.

The more common method is the separate body and frame process, in which the body is built as an entity and then mounted on the chassis. Most U.S. cars used this method.

In either type of body construction there are both inner and outer body panels, made of stamped steel. Normally the inner panels are made of heavier gauge metal, providing more strength

The last U.S. four-door convertible used unitized body and frame construction. Continentals are rigid and strong. Look for rust along rocker panels and wheel arches. Check center post.

than the outer stampings, or "body skin." The inner stampings often serve more than one make of car, with the visible outer skin panels sometimes being somewhat different to provide styling differences between the makes.

These inner and outer steel stampings are welded together to provide the basic components of the body, such as the cowl section, doors, rear panels, deck lids, etc. The various components are welded to each other to form the body. Many body components used on convertibles were also used on other models.

Because convertibles lack a rigid roof, extra bracing is usually provided. The chassis frame, which is usually a three-sided channel, is closed in and reinforced by welding a fourth side, making it box shaped to give extra strength. Some manufacturers added an extra cross brace between the side members of the frame.

Open frame girders.

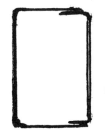

Closed or box girder frame.

100

Doors comprise an inner panel that is stamped and crimped for strength. Inside panel metal is bent to form the front and rear edge of the door. Outside skin is attached, and a flange hides the joint.

Additional bracing is usually provided in the cowl section between the fire wall and the front support for the doors. Additional bracing may be welded in place to give extra support to the upright against which the door hinges are attached. Sometimes extra bracing is added across the body near the opening of the rear deck.

We'll assume that you didn't buy a car that is badly dented and possibly out of line. Directions on body repairs will cover the type of dents often found in used cars, especially ones that may be up to twenty-five years old.

Auto body shops are equipped with power tools to straighten out the worst wrecks. Frame-straightening machines, power jacks, spreaders and metal stretchers are a few of the power tools auto body shops use. With this type of equipment a smashed body can be rebuilt. Information on this type of equipment will not be covered as it won't apply to the body work you'll do on your car.

Because of differences in body construction and assembly in the years following World War II, and variations among manufacturers, discussion and directions on body repair must be gen-

101

Handy assortment of tools necessary to handle most body and fender repairs. You can usually rent power tools you need. Saber saw isn't necessary
unless you have to cut out old metal.

eralized. You should gain the basic information you'll need from
the following pages. However, if you feel you need more specific
information on your particular car, write the manufacturer. For
cars that are no longer produced, sources of information can be
found in the bibliography.

Body repairs are easier to make when you have the right tools
and allow yourself plenty of working room. Depending upon the
extent of the body work you plan to do, you should buy (or borrow)
the following:

DOLLY BLOCKS: You'll need two or three of these hand-size
anvils in varying radii to conform to body curves. These are held
against one side of the metal while hammering against it. There
are no tricks to using these, and you'll get good results as long as
the dolly is held solidly against the metal that is being hammered.

HAMMERS: You'll need a heavy roughing hammer or a rubber-head mallet for initial straightening, and two or three dinging hammers. Choose three- to six-inch head length, depending upon working room. Square heads are for work close to seams and joints; round heads are for general work. The flat face is better for large areas, the crowned face for curved metal. The pointed end, or pick hammer, is for small dents. When using dinging hammers, be sure to choose the hammer with the head designed for the job you're doing, as explained above. To get the most force from each hammer stroke, grasp the handle at the end. Don't use these hammers for driving nails or tacks; keep them for body work only.

PRY BARS: Also known as pick tools. Choose one with a pointed end, the other with a flat or forked end. These are used to reach behind bracing bars and brackets to pry metal back into shape. Be sure to pry squarely against the metal so you won't stretch it out of shape at the edge of the pry bar.

SPOONS: Choose two or three in various shapes. They're a multipurpose tool used as dolly blocks to hammer against in close areas and to pry metal back into shape. When you're using a spoon as an anvil, be sure it is flat against the metal so hammer blows will shape the metal as you wish. When used for prying, be sure it is squarely against the metal so you won't stretch the pried metal out of shape.

ELECTRIC HAND DRILL: Not absolutely necessary but very handy. Use it for grinding, sanding and polishing, in addition to drilling holes. An assortment of bits from $\frac{1}{16}$ to $\frac{9}{16}$ inches should suffice. Buy the disc sander-grinder attachment, as well as an abrasive wheel and cone-shape mandrel. You'll need a packet of assorted abrasive discs. A stiff wire brush wheel will also be very useful.

FILE HOLDER AND FILES: Choose the flexible holder that allows adjustment to fit body curves. Two or three flexible files in assorted cuts will be needed. When using a file, remember to apply even pressure so you remove equal amounts of metal from the area you're filing.

PULL RODS: Sometimes called pull hooks. These hardened steel hooks allow you to pull metal back into shape where there isn't room enough to use a hammer and dolly. These are especially helpful for creases in doors and deck lids. For best use, drill a series of small holes, insert the rod and pull straight toward you.

SABER SAW: If you have a lot of old metal to cut out, a small electric saber saw or jigsaw will be handy. Buy an assortment of blades, from fine to coarse. For small amounts of metal you can usually use a hand saber saw, a hacksaw or tin snips. Be sure to buy the saw with the three-prong cord for safety. When using the saw, hold the guide plate flat against the metal you're cutting.

VICE GRIP PLIERS: You'll find a lot of uses for this handy tool: It's great for holding pieces of metal in the proper position for welding, or when drilling holes through two pieces of metal. Remember to hold it flat against the pieces as you tighten the thumbscrew.

HACKSAW: A sturdy hacksaw with an assortment of blades will be very useful. Get the kind that can adjust to hold blades vertically or horizontally. Keep the blade tight when you saw, and use a drop of oil on the metal you're cutting.

WIRE BRUSH: You'll find this very handy for cleaning away rust and scale, as well as for cleaning threads on bolts. Scrub flat against the object you're cleaning for best results. Sometimes sparks will fly as you use a wire brush, so be careful around solvents.

TIN SHEARS: You should have both the straight-cut and curve-cut blades if you'll be doing much metal work. The longer the handles, the more leverage you'll get. Cut keeping the metal as close to the inside of the shears as possible.

You can locate all of these tools in hardware stores, automotive supply stores or through mail-order houses. Don't hesitate to ask the salesperson for advice if you're not sure about any tool.

In addition to these tools, you'll need a general assortment of hand tools for disassembling body parts. You can probably use the same tools you used for the mechanical restoration. None of the tools suggested are overly expensive, so get good quality ones to do the job properly and to avoid injury. Be sure electric-powered tools are grounded. Also be sure solvents and flammable liquids are stored in safe containers. You should also have a hand-type fire extinguisher, for grinding and welding operations often cause

When replacing floor metal, fit the drive shaft hump separately and weld in place. Side floor panels should be welded to all sides. Use rust-inhibiting primer on any old metal left in place.

sparks to fly. Use caution and good sense as you work on your convertible.

To repair rust-through spots on floors and body panels, the following procedures will do the job, and you should have no difficulty:

Scrape surrounding areas free of rust and scale with a wire brush, or with your hand drill's wire brush wheel attachment. Be sure you scrape or grind until you find solid metal.

Outline the area to be cut out with chalk, a soapstone marker or a felt-tip pen. Be sure to mark on solid metal. You'll find it easier to fit pieces of new metal if you make the outline generally rectangular rather than curved.

Drill a $\%_{16}$-inch hole in each corner, and two or three holes on each side of the corner hole along the cut line. To keep the drill from "wandering," make a slight indentation with a prick punch or sharp nail where each hole is to be drilled. When drilling holes, be sure you don't drill into any tubing, wires or mechanisms behind the metal.

After drilling, cut out the rusted metal following the outline. You'll find it easier to start the cut at the corners, leaving bottom metal to act as a brace as you cut. Use a hand or electric saber

Measure areas to be cut out and outline them with chalk. When cutting floors, take care not to cut or damage brake lines, muffler, gas tank or other parts below the floor. Use hacksaw, snips or saber saw.

You can usually remove a damaged wheel well by cutting rivets with a cold chisel. If it's welded in place you'll have to cut it out. Be careful not to cut your hands on sharp edges—work gloves help.

saw, and tin shears. Make the cut slowly so it will be exact with even edges.

When you've cut out the old metal, and before cutting new metal to fit, make a pattern on a piece of cardboard. Hold the cardboard behind the hole and trace along the edges. If you're going to have new metal welded in, you can cut replacement metal along the pattern lines and have it ready for the welder. If you're going to attach the patch yourself and not have the metal welded in, trace the pattern on the new metal, then allow about an inch extra on each measurement and draw in the new lines, which will make the patch metal larger than the hole it is to cover. Cut along the outside lines with your saber saw, hacksaw or tin shears.

If the new piece of metal is to be welded in place, hold it with the vice grip pliers to be certain it doesn't move during the process.

If you're going to insert the new metal as a patch, and you have cut the piece larger than the hole as directed, make a series of

When installing a new floor in the storage compartment, leave holes for bolts that hold the gas tank in place. Be sure to drill a hole in the bottom of the tire well so any water that leaks in can drain out. Prime the area.

You can replace any portion of a body panel. Cut out old metal and weld in replacement purchased from wrecking yard. When weld seam is ground smooth, replacement won't show if properly painted.

marks about two inches apart around the perimeter of the patch area. Use a punch or sharp nail to make a slight indentation, and drill a ³⁄₁₆-inch hole at each mark. Line up the metal to be used as a patch behind the area, and mark through the holes to indicate where each corner hole is to be drilled in the patch metal. Using a reaming bit, ream each hole so the slot-headed bolt will fit flush into the hole. Insert and tighten the slot-headed bolts in each corner. Working in each direction from each corner, punch or drill the holes in the patch metal (already in place). As you drill a hole, insert and tighten the slot-headed bolt to hold the metal securely as you work on the next hole. It is much better to use ³⁄₁₆-inch bolts close to each other than larger bolts farther apart.

Remember, this method of installing your own patch metal behind the cutout metal is only for areas that are not structural supports. Weakness in a structural part requires new metal welded in place for safety and strength.

As you become proficient at cutting and fitting metal, you may feel you can skip the pattern-making step. In this case, trace the outline of the hole directly on the metal you're going to use.

A beginning restorer should have welding done by a professional. However, if you feel you want to learn how to weld, books on the subject are available; one is listed in the bibliography at the back of this book.

When new metal is welded in place, grind down the weld seam with an abrasive disc on your drill. Final filing with a hand file will smooth the seam, making it ready for finishing. Fill any low

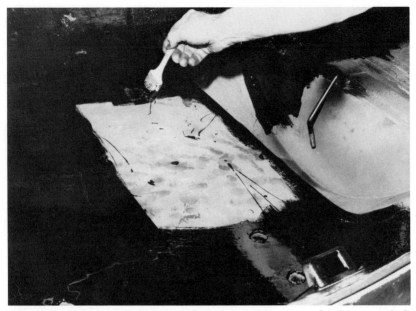

After priming new metal, coat with undercoating or regular home asphalt roofing paint, which deadens sound as well as preserves the metal. Let it dry thoroughly before installing carpet or matting.

spots in the seam with a good grade of body putty or epoxy filler, then sand smooth before applying a coat of primer paint. Take each new metal insert to the priming stage to prevent rusting. Leave final finishing for your last step before painting.

Essentially the same steps should be taken for repairing rust-through spots in fenders and fender panels. This metal should be welded in place rather than fitting a patch piece as described earlier. However, because of the crown or curve in many fenders, you may have some additional steps to follow in fitting the replacement metal. Take the time necessary to measure, cut and fit the piece to be used as a replacement. Once one edge of the metal is welded in place, the welder can heat and hammer the rest to conform to any crown or curve in the fender.

If the fender is dented as well as containing rust-through areas, pound out the dent first. Always work from the outer edge of the dent toward the point of impact for best results, and to avoid stretching the metal out of shape. First determine the point of impact, then trace the damage through to the outer edges. You can

A fender as badly rusted as on this Valiant Signet will be easier to replace than repair. A fender from a Valiant sedan or station wagon will fit. The rust damage can be repaired if you can't locate a replacement.

usually find the point of impact by a deep scratch or tear in the metal. The ripples or ridges that form from this point must be hammered out first, starting at the outer edge.

In most cases you can leave the fender on the car during the repair job. The advantages are that you're less apt to change the crown or curve of the metal if it is solidly attached to the car. The amount of work room you have with the fender in place will usually be the determining factor. In many cases you'll need the extra swinging room you get by removing the wheel. If you do remove the wheel, be sure to use a properly placed jack stand to support the car's weight. At the rear, the jack stand should usually be positioned where the spring is attached to the axle, unless there is a jack pad built in. At the front the best support place for the jack stand will be where the front spring is cradled in the wheel support arms, where a jack pad may be provided. Many restorers like to place the jack stands under a flat area on the chassis frame rather than on the axle or spring mount. In any case, be sure it is securely placed so no amount of pounding will jar the car off the stand.

If the dent is large or severe, first use your roughing hammer or rubber mallet to pound out the worse indentations and generally shape the metal. Choose a hand dolly that most closely approximates the curve of the metal. Use the crowned head hammer with a round face. Start at the outer edge of the dent and hammer against the metal, bracing with the dolly on the opposite side. Hammer small areas at a time, moving along the line of the dent toward the point of impact. It may take several hammering operations before the metal is back in shape. It is better to hammer a little of the dent out and move along the line of the dent, rather than to try and get the metal completely back in shape at the first hammering. You should hammer on the outside of the metal with the dolly inside, unless it is easier for you to do the opposite because of the swinging room of the hammer.

Torn metal should be welded after the dents are removed to the point where the torn edges meet. After welding, the dents can again be hammered and the metal smoothed. In some cases you may want to reinforce the fender by having a patch welded in place behind the tear, and the edges of the tear butt-welded. This extra strength can help prevent the metal from tearing from vibrations and metal fatigue. With the dents removed and any torn metal welded together, you can grind, file, sand and prime the area as previously described.

Spots where rust has eaten through the fender or fender panel must be cut out. It is a mistake to simply fill these spots with plastic filler, repaint them and consider them repaired.

Cracks in a corner of body metal must be thoroughly examined to find the cause. Cracked metal should be welded, or strengthened by welding in a patch on the underside. Don't use plastic filler.

Properly applied, a fiberglass patch is fine for nonstructural repairs as on this Valiant. When properly sanded and primed it's ready for primer. Sand prime coats smooth before applying the finish coat.

On relatively small rust-through areas around the headlights or turn signals, or at the bottom of the fender, some restorers prefer to cut out the rusted metal, fill the area with a fiberglass cloth and coat it with epoxy resin mixed with hardener. This easy method gives satisfactory results for areas that are not structural. It's also very handy for areas difficult to reach and work with other tools.

When using fiberglass, the area must be thoroughly cleaned, with all scale and rust removed. A solvent or detergent is necessary to remove oil film, wax, etc. Drill several small holes in the good metal around the area so the epoxy resin will get a firm hold. Cut the fiberglass cloth a couple of inches larger than the area it is to cover. In some cases you may need several layers of cloth. If so, cut each layer slightly larger than the previous piece to strengthen the patch. If a fairly large hole or area is being covered, wadded steel wool or paper can be stuffed in to support the cloth until the resin dries. The metal should be fairly warm—at least 70 degrees —to insure proper adhesion of the epoxy resin. A heat lamp, electric space heater or infrared lamp on an extension cord will

To repair damage to rear panel of this Monterey, remove name plate, bump metal out from the inside, and smooth with dinging hammer and hand dolly. File any high spots and use epoxy filler on low spots.

usually suffice. Be careful not to let any of the resin or hardener touch the lamp or contact the source of heat.

You should have no difficulty in working with fiberglass. Be sure to mix the resin and hardener in a flat glass pan according to directions furnished with the materials. The exact proportion of hardener to resin is very important, both for strength and to determine the amount of time you have to work with it before it sets up. Be sure to wear gloves while mixing and working with these materials. Cut the cloth to the right dimensions, dip it in the mixture, then apply it over the area and smooth it tightly against the surface. Apply as many layers as you feel necessary, one right after the other. You can apply additional resin-hardener mix with a rubber squeegee over the patch as needed. Allow the area to dry thoroughly before sanding and priming.

To repair doors and deck lids with large rust-through areas, scrape away the rust and scaled metal until you reach solid metal. In those cases where the rust-out goes to the bottom edge of the door or lid, scrape away what you can, then mark the area to be cut away above it. You'll have to set the cut on your saber saw, or use a shorter blade if the cut isn't adjustable, so you won't hit the inner bracing panel as you cut. Remove the weakened metal and cut new metal to fit. Make a cardboard pattern first, if this will help you. You may have to plan on the new metal extending over the old metal along the bottom to give necessary strength. This shouldn't extend to the point where it will alter the alignment of the panels, nor prevent a proper fit.

Normally there is space of about ¼ to ½ inch between the bottom of the door and the rocker panel. There is about the same amount of space between the bottom of the deck lid and the panel to which it closes. This room allows for slight extension of the replacement metal if necessary to gain needed strength. Proper filing and finishing of the door or deck lid and the rocker panel will hide any additional thickness of metal.

If the rust-through is far enough above the bottom edge of the door or deck lid so there is solid metal left in place after cutting out the weak metal, have new metal welded in place as previously described.

Many times there will be crease marks and dents on doors, panels and deck lids that haven't cut through the metal, and around which there may be only light surface rust. In these cases you

Small dents, as on this Mercury, can be bumped out from the inside and finished with a dinging hammer. If color will be hard to match, paint the entire panel. Mask off chrome trim and cover the wheel.

Lack of working space makes it necessary to either weld new metal over the dent in the rocker panel or drill a series of holes and use pull hooks. Door dent can be bumped back in place from inside.

can usually repair them by using the pull rods described in the list of tools.

Use a solvent or detergent to clean away road film and wax. Make a series of 9/64-inch holes about half an inch apart along the deepest line of the crease. Be careful not to drill deep enough to cut through anything inside the door. Starting at the end opposite the point of impact, insert the pull rods and pull the metal out slightly. You may want to use one hook, tapping with the crowned dinging hammer as you pull the metal back in shape. Work toward the point of impact, planning on going back to the first hole and starting over when you finish the first series of pulls.

If the point of impact is in the middle and the crease runs in two or more directions from the center point, work from each edge, a couple of holes at a time. This way, the metal may almost spring back into place as you approach the center point.

With the creases removed, fill the drill holes with plastic filler, then sand and prime until they no longer show. Holding a light at an angle from the crease will show ripples that need to be filled to make the job perfect.

As previously mentioned, doors and other body panels are made up of an outer skin and an inner bracing panel that is welded to it. Because of body contours and strengthening crimps made into the bracing panels, there is often only an inch or two between the inner

115

Small dents in a deck lid, as on this Rambler American, can sometimes be bumped out from inside. Because of the small space between panels, it's often easier to drill a few holes and use pull hooks, then fill.

and outer panels. In these cases you may find it impossible to remove some dents. If there is room, try pry bars and spoons, as previously described. Pull bars can also be used. If you decide to use a spoon and an anvil to hammer against, choose a crowned-head, round-face dinging hammer. If these methods don't bring the metal back into shape, drill holes and fill with epoxy resin, as other creases. Once sanded and primed, it will finish out satisfactorily, with the dents and creases hidden.

There are several excellent brands of plastic body fillers available. Each contains directions for mixing. After cleaning the area thoroughly, sanding away any surface rust, feathering the surrounding edges and using a coarse grit sandpaper to roughen the dented area, you're ready for the plastic filler. Use a putty knife to mix the resin and catalyst as directed on a piece of flat glass. Apply with a rubber or plastic squeegee over the dented area. It's better to use several light coats, allowing drying time between each, rather than one thick coat. When the plastic has set firmly it can be sanded and primed, and will make a very satisfactory job.

Occasionally you'll come across metal that has been dented or stretched from the inside, causing a bulge on the outside skin. Or you may find by using the wrong combination of dinging hammer and dolly you've stretched the outer skin. When you discover areas of stretched metal, you'll have to shrink the metal back into shape.

There are three methods to shrink metal. You can apply heat from a torch, then use a dolly and hammer to pound the metal back into shape. If you decide on this method, heat the spot at the center of the bulge, then hammer against the dolly. While heating and hammering the center spot, continue the process around the area in a circular fashion until the additional metal is hammered down. You can only use this method when there is room to hold the dolly behind the area against which you're hammering. It may be helpful to ask someone to hold the dolly on the inside so you can continue to apply heat from the torch as you hammer. Be careful, of course, not to start a fire in any body insulation or other materials when you use a torch.

Another method used by restorers to shrink metal is a shrinking hammer and a dolly. The shrinking hammer wasn't described along with the other dinging hammers. Its face has crisscross grooves, somewhat similar to the kind of mallet used to tenderize tough meat. By hammering against a dolly, the metal is shrunk back into its original shape. This process will leave small crisscross marks in the metal, which must be sanded and filled before priming. It is by far the easiest of the three methods for a beginning restorer.

A third method is to cut a narrow slit, or series of slits, in the bulged metal, then hammer them into an overlapping position to shrink the metal. They are then welded, the weld seam is countersunk by hammering, and the surface is ground smooth before being filled, if necessary, sanded and primed.

If you have to contend with stretched metal, try whichever method you feel will be easiest for the particular job. Remember the fire-hazard problem with the torch, especially if the metal you must shrink is near the gas tank.

After completing the body work of repairing rust-through areas with new metal or fiberglass, and straightening out dents and creases in the body and fenders, check the alignment of doors, deck lid and hood to be sure they fit as originally intended. When properly aligned, the space between the door and adjoining panels to the front and rear should be equal. This should be from ⅛ to ¼ of an inch. The clearance between the bottom of the door and the rocker panel may be ¼ inch or more, but it should be the same distance from the panel for the whole length of the door.

The deck lid should be centered in the opening provided for it, with equal distances between the lid and the surrounding panels. The distance between the lid and the panel against which it closes at the bottom may be more than the distance between the lid and the sides, but it should be the same distance all across the bottom. On the sides and top the lid should be about ⅛ of an inch. The rubber seal against which the lid closes provides the necessary seal against water leakage.

Proper alignment of doors, deck lid and hood are important safety factors, since none should jar open as the car is driven. They must open and close easily, without extra force having to be applied. If properly aligned, and if the rubber seals are in good condition, they won't rattle when closed. Proper closure is especially important on convertibles since the doors provide the only support for the windows. If doors are correctly aligned, the win-

Wire grinding wheel in electric hand drill helps remove rust and scale from channels in which weather stripping will fit. After area is cleaned, prime and paint before installing new weather stripping.

dows will fit correctly, making them less apt to rattle and assuring maximum weather protection with the folding top supports. The beginning restorer can make these adjustments easily.

There are provisions for aligning doors fore and aft, up and down, as well as in and out, assuring correct fit.

Unless the hinges have been bent in a collision—and this is unlikely as they're of heavier material than the metal into which they're attached—doors can generally be positioned while on the car. It may require someone's help to hold the door in position while you tighten the holding bolts. You may find it easier to adjust these bolts if you first squirt them with a little penetrating oil or kerosene. Use a box-end or socket wrench with a ratchet attachment to adjust these bolts.

The in-or-out adjustments are usually provided on the part of the hinge that attaches to the door. The bolts extend through elongated slots in the door and tighten into threaded anchor plates inside the door. Loosen the holding bolts in the door side of one hinge and position the door. Tighten the bolts on this hinge before loosening the bolts on the other hinge. Normally it's easier to position the bottom hinge first. On your first try you may find you have to go back and make a second adjustment to the bottom hinge after positioning the top hinge.

To change the up-or-down position of the doors, loosen the holding bolts where the hinges are attached to the upright body support. This will be at the cowl on most cars, on the rear upright support on those few cars with the doors hinged at the back.

To make this adjustment you must loosen the holding bolts in both hinges, for you can't move the door up or down if only one hinge has been loosened. In a few cases you may need to use a pry bar to lift the door and hold it in position while you tighten the bolts, because of the weight of the door. A friend's help here is very handy. To gauge the distance the door must be raised or lowered before you loosen any bolts, check how the moldings line up with adjoining panels. Mark this distance with a pencil above the hinge on the support post. Then, after loosening the hinges, move the hinge up to your mark.

The front-to-back position of the door is usually controlled by the use of shims where the hinge attaches to the upright support.

Narrow shims can be added to move the door toward the rear, and shims can be removed to move the door forward. Work on one hinge at a time. You can gauge the distance the door must be moved in either direction by measuring the distance between the edge of the door and the adjoining body panels.

Occasionally you'll come across a door that seems to be improperly hung and is unevenly placed in the door opening. If the top rear edge of the door is below the level of the adjoining panel, shims must be added to the lower hinge or removed from the upper hinge. If the top rear edge of the door is above the level of the adjoining panel, shims must be removed from the lower hinge or added to the top hinge, taking into consideration the front-to-back position of the door.

When making any adjustments on doors, also check the adjustment of the striker pin or catch against which the latch closes. The latch should center on the holding device. If you changed the position of the door, spread some grease lightly on the striker pin or plate. When the latch closes against it, the marks on the grease will indicate what, if any, adjustments should be made. If you have to move the latch up or down, in or out, be sure you tighten it securely after moving it. After adjusting door latches, striker pin and door catch, apply a little powdered graphite to lubricate these parts.

Door adjustments on four-door convertibles are made the same way as on two-door models. However, a change in a front or rear door on the same side may necessitate a change in the other door on the same side to make moldings line up properly. Work one side completely, front and rear doors, before adjusting doors on the other side of the car.

Before you consider door adjustments complete, raise the windows and check how they line up with the windshield and other windows, as well as with the weather stripping on the folding top rails. If the top of the windows do not fit against the weather stripping on the folding top rails, or if the top of the windows don't fit snugly against the weather stripping on the windshield post, this indicates that the top hinge is out of line and has positioned the top of the door too far out. Conversely, if the top of the window binds or fits under instead of snugly against the weather stripping, or binds against the weather stripping near the top of the windshield post, this indicates the top of the door is in too close and must be moved out to correct the condition.

Should you have to remove a door, you generally have two choices. Either remove the holding bolts on the door and remove the door by itself, leaving the hinges on the support post, or remove the holding bolts on the upright support and remove the door complete with hinges. Do whichever is more convenient for you, depending upon the job you're going to perform. There will usually be a rod that keeps the door from opening too far and straining the hinges; this must be disconnected by removing a small bolt or cotter pin.

If your car has power windows, be sure to disconnect the electric lines before removing the door. Some cars have cigarette lighters, lights, or other electrically operated devices in the doors. The wires to these must be disconnected and labeled before the door is removed.

When repairing electric windows, you'll find the connections just under the control switches. Mark which switch controls each window by referring to control plate. Be careful not to damage insulation.

If motor works, check holding bolts of window crank mechanism. Be sure teeth in gears aren't mashed or bent. Clean accumulated dirt from mechanism and spray with a lubricating solvent.

If you have to replace window glass there is no need to remove the door. On most cars, if you remove the molding at the top of the door you can run the window up beyond its normal top position. Then the arms that slide in grooves at the bottom of the window glass can be slipped through, allowing you to lift the glass out of the door. The same method applies to rear quarter windows. Normally vent window glass can be removed by turning the vent all the way open, removing any rear frame or screw that goes through the glass near the pivot points, and pulling the glass back and out. Windshield glass is normally replaced by removing inside moldings as well as outside moldings, peeling out any weather stripping or freeing the glass from the weather stripping by forcing a thin blade or putty knife under the glass, and freeing the glass from that portion of the weather stripping that folds over it. Because of the size of most windshields, you'll find they have a sealer or cement around the back edge of the glass against the weather stripping. This may require you to push the windshield forward with some force from inside the car after you've freed it of the overlap on the weather stripping.

122

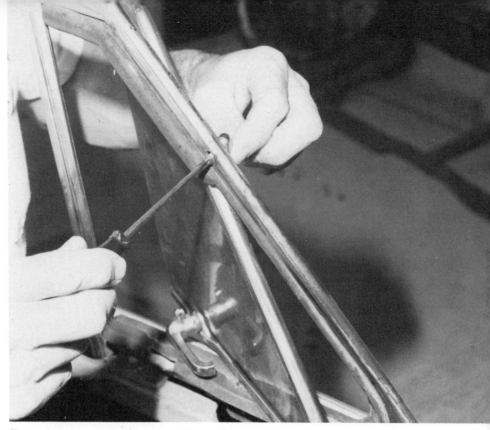

Removing a screw in the upper hinge allows vent window to be taken from frame. Bolt into door framework holds vent in place. With nut removed, vent window lifts up and out of frame. Handle rubber seals with care.

If you're going to install the new glass yourself rather than having it done at an auto glass shop, remember to handle the glass carefully. Plan to use a flat surface, and cover this surface with a towel or small piece of carpet to avoid scratching the glass. Clean the channel into which the glass fits, and use new stripping. Place the frame into which the glass fits against a solid edge. Put some sealer or cement along the metal frame, and press the stripping into it. Some prefer to wrap the stripping over the edge of the glass and tap both into place together. In either case, use a rubber mallet, and tap gently. Sometimes a small piece of wood inserted between the top of the glass and the mallet will distribute the force of the blow evenly, making the glass fit into the channel easier.

Because of size, windshields are somewhat harder to handle. There are some tips that will make the job less difficult, however. Clean out the area against which the weather seal is to fit, and

Side and door windows go into place through top of the door or side panel. Remove window molding, wind glass all the way up, remove spring clips and slip ends of control arms through slots.

coat it with cement. Usually you should install new weather stripping with a new windshield. Put a thin coat of sealer on the edge of the weather stripping that will fit against the glass. It's normally easier to insert the bottom of the glass in the weather strip channel. Before you attempt to force the glass into the remaining weather stripping, cut two pieces of string long enough to tie to something at the center of the dashboard or console. These strings should extend from the object to which they're tied, through the windshield opening, and well over the new glass. As you force the new glass into the weather strip channel, the string will be between the glass and the weather stripping. Pull the string along the edge of the glass and it will force the edge of the weather stripping over the glass, seating the glass perfectly. Untie the strings and pull them out when the glass is completely in place.

Use wire-bristled brush to clean rust and scale from the track on which the lowering/raising arms ride. Spray with lubricating solvent to keep the mechanism operating properly.

Usually bolts or screws hold the window frame together. On convertibles without framed windows, only the channel at the bottom holds the glass in place. Be sure both channel and framework are clean.

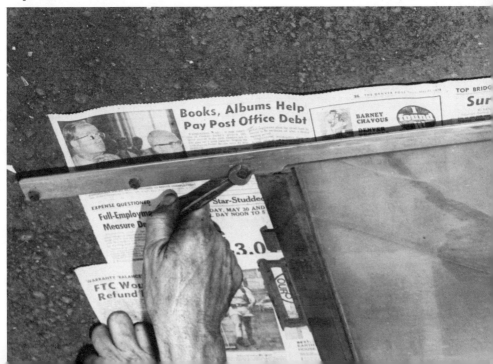

Hood panels and rear decks can be adjusted for correct alignment in two ways. On hoods hinged at the cowl (this is the method used on most U.S.-made cars for the last thirty years) there are two elongated holes on the fire wall. One of these controls the side-to-side positioning of the hinge. An elongated hole in the portion of the hinge that attaches to the fire wall controls the up-and-down hinge position. Loosen one side at a time, position it correctly and tighten it before working on the other side.

The front-to-back adjustment of the hood is changed by loosening the bolts holding the hinge to the hood panel. Elongated holes allow the panel to be moved to the front or back when the holding bolts are loosened. Loosen both sides, position the hood correctly and tighten the bolts.

After repositioning the hood, check the alignment of the hood latch and holding pin or catch at the front to be sure it lines up properly. Rubber bumpers on threaded studs at each side of the

Elongated slots in trunk and hood panels allow hinge to move for proper alignment. When lining up doors, hood or deck lid, tighten only one bolt per side until alignment and fit is correct.

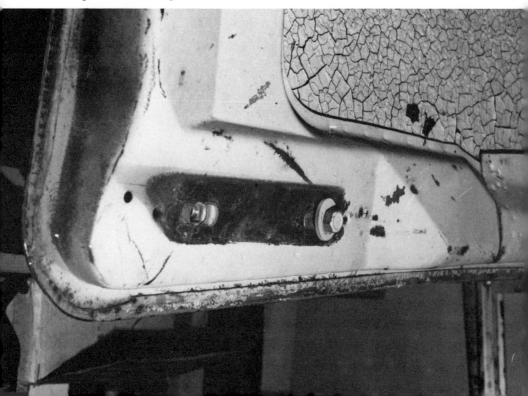

hood or striker panel can be adjusted up or down to prevent hood flutter.

On hoods hinged at the front and closing against the cowl, the procedure is essentially the same. The up-or-down position is adjusted where the hinge attaches to the cross support, not on the hood panel. The front-to-back adjustment is made where the hinge attaches to the hood. The catch is usually on the fire wall, and the pin on the hood. When adjusting hood position, check the operation of the release mechanism to be sure it is securely attached and properly adjusted.

To position the deck lid from side to side, loosen the bolts holding the lid to the hinge. Elongated holes allow the panel to be moved to center it in the deck opening. Loosen both sides, then tighten after the lid is properly positioned. Elongated holes in the lid permit movement of the lid fore and aft. You can usually gauge how much you need to move the lid from side to side or front to back to get proper positioning before you loosen any holding bolts.

To make the leading edge of the deck lid level with the body panel, shims may be added between the hinge and the deck lid, though some cars provide for this adjustment by elongated holes in the body panel against which the hinge attaches. If you repositioned the deck lid, check to see how the latch mates with the catch on the bottom panel. Be sure they mate securely, and that the holding bolts are tight. Usually the lock only prevents the handle from turning, so you just need to make sure the holding bolts are tight and the locking bar moves freely.

Remember that the springs holding the hood and deck lid open will be under tension. Carefully release the tension on these springs. Use pliers to pull the curved end of the spring out of the connecting hole, and release the tension gradually. Some cars have a hinged rod that holds hood or deck lid in place when opened. Check how these are attached to the hood or lid, and that the attachment is secure. The holes or notches into which these rods fit to hold the lid open usually require no attention. Cars that use a sliding arm within a casing, with a ratchet device that holds the arm in position, usually require only light lubrication with powdered graphite or oil unless the ratchet device has bent.

While you're working on the body there are some simple steps you can take to prevent future body rot and deterioration. Clean the inside of the door panels with a wire brush—you may have to remove insulating panels to do the job properly. With all the scale and rust removed, coat the area with a rust-inhibiting primer. You may want to spray on undercoating before replacing the insulation. Normally the insulation will stick to the still-wet undercoating; if not, use some mastic.

You can prevent future deterioration of the fenders and fender panels by removing all dirt, scale, rust, etc. Pay particular attention to the crimped or rolled metal at the bottom of fenders and wheel arches, since these are the areas where dirt collects and holds moisture. After removing all you can with a wire brush and putty knife, wash the area with kerosene or a commercial grease remover. Be careful not to inhale the fumes. After this, wash the area with a strong detergent-and-water solution, and rinse with clear water. When dry, apply a coat of rust-inhibiting primer and finish with spray-on undercoating.

Clean out the rocker panels that are open on the side toward the car's frame, and those that have a turned-back or rolled-back edge for stiffening. Use the same procedures as for the underside of fenders to give lasting protection. On boxed-in rocker panels, be sure the drain holes are open so water won't be trapped inside. The drain holes at the bottom of side panels and on doors must be free of obstructions that would hold dirt and would trap moisture.

Proper sealing around the windshield and cowl ventilators will keep water from running inside the cowl panel. There are many excellent sealers that are easily applied between the glass and rubber seal, as well as between the rubber weather stripping and the body. Of course you want good weather stripping around doors, deck lid and where the top joins the windshield.

The areas around headlights, parking lights, turn signals and rear lights can be protected from the inside by a thorough cleaning, removal of any rust or scale, and a protective coat of rust-inhibiting primer and undercoating. Any rubber grommets around openings in the body must be complete and properly seated if they're to seal out dust and water.

You can protect body metal by coating inside panels with asphalt roofing paint. This is less expensive than spray-on undercoating, and lasts better. If applying insulation, do it before paint dries.

Use wire-bristled brush to remove rust and scale from channel where top joins body, as well as around deck or hood openings. After cleaning the area, use a rust-inhibiting primer before any color coat.

If the rear compartment is lined, remove the lining and clean the inside of the body panels. Rust-inhibiting paint will prevent future deterioration. The drain hole at the bottom of the spare wheel well must be open to allow drainage. The rubber weather stripping around the deck lid should be complete, in place, with enough resiliency to compress when the lid is closed against it. New weather stripping isn't expensive and is readily available to fit most cars.

Be sure the fabric top on your convertible overlaps the body at areas where it's attached. This will shed water on the outside of the body, keeping it from draining into body panels and upholstery.

The car's paint job will protect the body on the outside. Thorough cleaning and coating with rust-inhibiting paint and undercoating will additionally protect the inside of the body, keeping it strong and serviceable for years. Using care, a beginning restorer can perform all these tasks without difficulty.

6

An Inside Job

With the body and fender repairs completed, it's time to concentrate on the inside of your convertible. Much of the enjoyment and pride of owning your car depends upon the appearance of the interior.

Normally it's easier to work on the interior before you concentrate on the roof, for you'll have more room to move seats, panels, etc. in and out of the car without having to worry about damage to the roof. However, if you prefer you can repair or replace the roof first, then work on the inside.

You can probably do whatever is necessary to restore the seats, upholstery panels, carpets and interior trim items to like-new condition. It's not necessary to have this work done by an auto trim shop, except in very unusual cases, unless you want to. A home sewing machine will work fine for stitching all but the heaviest leather upholstery.

Some convertibles used leather for all or parts of seats, as well as on side panels. If your car is one of these, you'll probably want to keep it in leather. There is no problem obtaining leather in several grades, and almost any color you want. Later, moderately priced convertibles used vinyl upholstery throughout; the more expensive ones used leather for seat facings, matching vinyl for other parts. In most cases you can match the color and pattern originally used. If not, you may want to consider a contrasting color or pattern.

You'll find it easier to work on cushions, panels, carpets, etc. if you remove these from the car to a workbench or other flat surface. Be sure the work surface is clean and free from nails or sharp protrusions.

To extricate upholstery panels, remove any plated screws and lift off the molding at the top of the panel. On some cars there may be clips behind the moldings and screws on the ends that only show when the doors are opened. Some window cranks are attached by Allen-head bolts, or by screws that must be removed before the crank can be pulled off the shaft. Others have a decorative escutcheon plate; press it back to expose the tapered pin, which must be driven out. A few manufacturers used a clip that required the panel to be pushed against the door, so the spring clip can be removed.

Most door handles are attached the same way as window cranks, and must be removed before the upholstery panel can be taken off. The small push buttons that operate the door locks can be unscrewed, whether they extend through the molding or the panel. When removing door hardware, be sure to save any washers, springs, pins, screws, etc. as you'll need them later.

The armrests on the doors of some cars are held in place by screws in the underside of the armrest. These must be removed before the armrest can be lifted off. On other cars the armrest is attached only to the upholstery panel and will come off with the panel. Ashtrays, hardware for adjusting mirrors, and any other attachment must be removed. Controls for electric windows and courtesy lights must be disconnected. Handle these very carefully to avoid damaging the wiring.

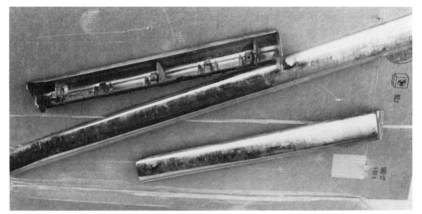

Screws and clips hold window moldings in place. A good scrubbing with detergent and water will usually clean up plated moldings. Painted trim parts are easy to refinish if properly sanded.

Many times soiled, dingy vinyl upholstery in convertibles will clean surprisingly well by scrubbing with a strong detergent-and-water solution or a commercial cleaner.

With the moldings and all hardware removed from the panel, look for plated screws that hold the panel in place. Once these are removed, locate the spring clips attached to the panel. These are hidden by the upholstery, and extend through the panel to fit into holes in the door. A thin blade or putty knife slid along the area between the panel and the door will indicate the location of these clips. When you locate one, pry gently against the panel to spring the clip out of the hole in the door. There may be as many as a dozen of these clips around the perimeter of the panel. With the clips pried carefully out of their holes, the panel should lift off. You may find that a plastic sheet has been installed as a water shield, protecting the upholstery backing panel and the window-operating mechanisms from water that can leak in when the windows are lowered or the rubber seal between the glass becomes badly worn. Be sure not to damage this plastic shield.

If no door repairs were necessary when you made body repairs, be sure to look at the drain holes in the bottom of the doors. They must be free of obstructions that could retain water inside the doors and cause rust.

Occasionally you'll find two panels on a door. The upper panel will usually extend about two-thirds of the way down and be covered with upholstery material. The lower panel may be covered

Once carpet scuff pad is cut and bound, spread household glue on the back to keep its tight fit. You may find that a few plated screws are used along the bottom edge, possibly one at the top edge of the pad.

Draw measurements on replacement fiberboard panel or door backing. Mark holes where window and door controls must be cut. Left and right door should be alike, but measure to make sure.

with carpet to act as a scuff pad. You can remove either or both, as required.

Upholstery panels are backed by fiberboard on most cars. The upholstery is stretched and glued to the fiberboard panel. However, the panels beside the rear seat that provide room for the folding top bows may be metal, with the upholstery glued in place. The thin cotton or foam padding will have to be replaced if the panel is in poor condition. Many times the bottom of the panel has rotted because of excessive and continuing moisture.

You may be able to repair the backing by fitting a piece of heavy cardboard to replace the rotted section, but only if the upholstery material itself doesn't need replacing. The fiberboard backing material is not expensive, so there's little to be gained by trying to splice in a partial section.

You can buy backing material in large sheets at auto trim shops or in building supply and some hardware stores. It is usually $\frac{3}{32}$- to $\frac{1}{8}$-inch thick. If possible, use the old piece for a pattern. Mark in the holes through which the spring clips are to be inserted, as well as the holes for the window crank, door handle, etc. Mark where screws for the armrest must penetrate the fiberboard. Because the backing is fairly heavy material, you will have difficulty cutting it with shears; use a coping saw with a fine blade. If the old panel is too badly deteriorated to use as a pattern, either take the measurements directly from the door or use the door panel on the opposite side. If you do take measurements from the opposite door, remember to "flip" the panel before recovering it.

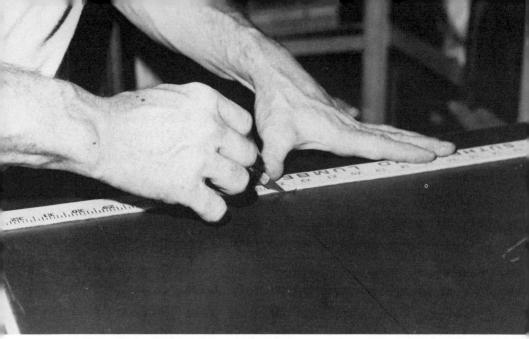

Use a sharp blade and a straight edge to cut along pattern marks. Fiber-board is usually too stiff to cut with tin snips. Mark holes where clips must fit, also holes for armrest supports.

Use chisel or knife to cut holes through which spring clips must fit to hold upholstery panel to door or side panel. Use pliers to push clips into place. Use tape as a backing piece.

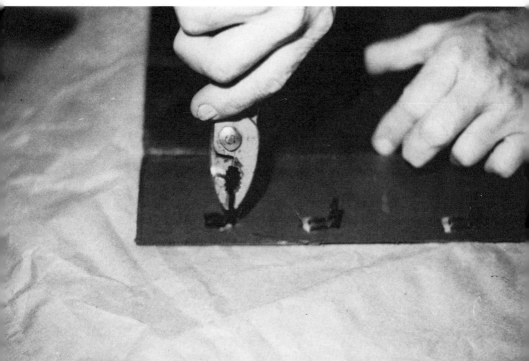

Although the manufacturer may not have done it, you may find it easier to hold the spring clips in place if you stretch a piece of heavy sealing tape over the back of them when they're in the proper position.

You should have no trouble recovering a door or side upholstery panel. To avoid drab appearance, there were usually seams that gave the effect of several pieces having been joined to make the panel. Others had two or more colors or patterns on each panel, while some had designs stitched in the material. If you want to keep your car as authentic as possible, follow the same color and decorating schemes used by the manufacturer.

If your's is a car on which one color or pattern was used on the entire panel, with seams sewn to make a design, cut the material sufficiently larger than the panel to allow an inch for each seam, and three inches on the overall outside dimensions. This will allow 1½ inches to turn back around each edge for gluing to the panel.

Be sure that the colors line up when installing cushions and side panels. A slotted hole on bottom of cushion allows for slight up-down positioning. Side and door panels can't be moved up or down.

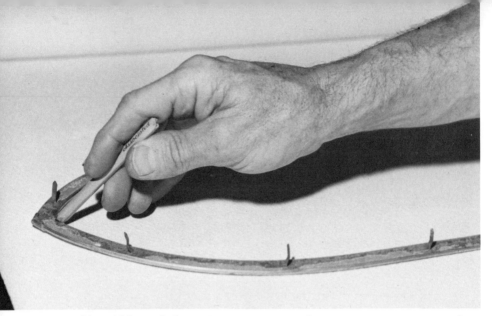

If panel has upholstery in two or more colors, you can trace pattern from molding strip. Allow extra material when cutting, but stitch along the line. Draw patterns on back of material.

When sewing seams into the material, notice how it was done on the original. In most cases the material is folded back against itself and sewn from the back side. Cording may be sewn into the seam, and is also used in some cars to separate panels as well as colors, and to accent certain areas. The cording may be the same color as the upholstery or may be a contrasting color.

Make cording by cutting the material into long strips. Cut on the bias if using cloth or a stretch material. The material should be wide enough to fold over the cording and to allow room for stitching, plus enough extra material for tacking, stapling or sewing into place. Buy the correct diameter cording at a trim shop or fabric shop. If you want cording that is greater in diameter than any you can locate, use plastic-covered clothesline or the correct diameter rope.

Fold the material over the cording and stitch, using the hinged zipper foot on a home sewing machine to help you sew close to the cording. For strength, use nylon thread (in a matching color). If you need pieces of cording longer than the strips you cut, sew two or more strips together, fold over the cording and stitch. You can make welting for use around the edges of panels the same way.

Vinyl binding can be sewn to carpet on a home sewing machine. Sew material face-to-face so stitches don't show when binding is turned back. Use no. 16 or 18 needle.

Lay separate pieces of upholstery material in correct position to be sure everything is right before stitching pieces together. Metal or plastic trim strips should be thoroughly cleaned for reuse.

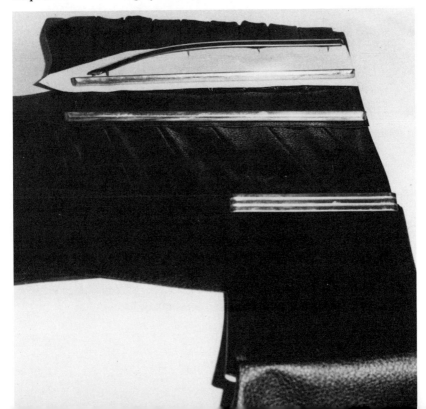

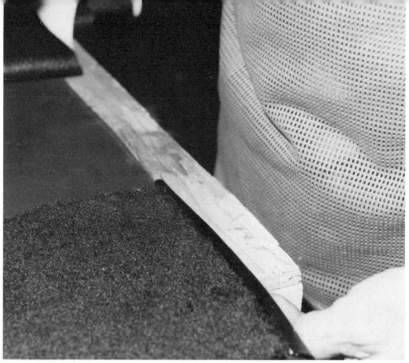

It's usually not necessary to bind the top edge of carpet scuff pad, for welting or binding on bottom of the upholstery gives the desired finished edge. The correct weight and color carpet is obtainable.

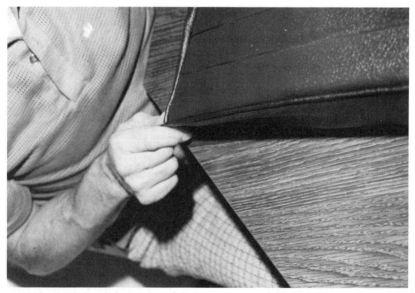

Stretch covering over framework so welting along the edge fits correctly. Take special care along front edge and sides: Excess material will be at back of cushion. Hand stitching may be necessary at back.

Fold the covering material back over itself before stitching to get a finished edge on both cording and welting. Some manufacturers used bright metal caps at ends of welting. Trim shops usually carry these.

If door and side panels have contrasting colors or fabrics, measure very carefully so these will line up properly when the panels are back in place.

If there is a decorative plated trim strip separating colors or patterns of upholstery fabrics, the strip must be removed so you can take the measurements for the new pieces. Metal trim pieces either clip into place, have prongs which go through the backing material and bend against it, or are held in place by small bolts. Trace the pattern these trim strips make, especially if they separate colors or patterns. You want all seams hidden by the decorative strip, so your measurements should be to the center of the strip. Allow extra material for seaming.

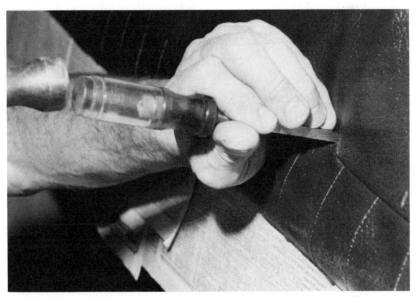

Measure and mark where slits must be made to hold clips attaching trim strips. A sharp chisel will do the job easily. Punch slits. Don't try to cut the material or you may make the slit too long.

You probably found lightweight backing material under the upholstery. This may tear apart when you remove the old material. You can buy this type padding material in trim shops, fabric shops and some department stores. You may want to consider substituting polyurethane or plastic foam for the original cotton padding, since these materials won't retain moisture like cotton padding.

You can cut the carpet necessary to make new scuff pads for the bottoms of panels. However, take care in cutting the carpet so you won't have loops or tufts pulling loose after the cut. To avoid raw edges, sew seaming tape around the edges or make some welting and sew this to the carpet, whichever matches the original pattern.

Sew upholstery materials from the back side so stitching won't show. Allow at least half an inch extra material outside the seam for strength. This can be trimmed closer if extra bulk would show.

You'll find that some of the seams and patterns sewn into panels appear to have been several pieces joined together. In most cases this seaming is done by folding the material back against itself and stitching to simulate a seam. Diamond-shape patterns are usually only stitched in rather than being separate pieces sewn together.

Though authenticity is worth striving for, remember that you're the one who will be using the car. Unless you plan to enter the car in shows, you have considerable leeway in what you do. One worthwhile change is to install carpet kickpads under the dashboard instead of the fiberboard ones commonly used. You can recover existing fiberboard kickboards if they're basically intact. Otherwise cut new ones and cover them with carpet. Take measure-

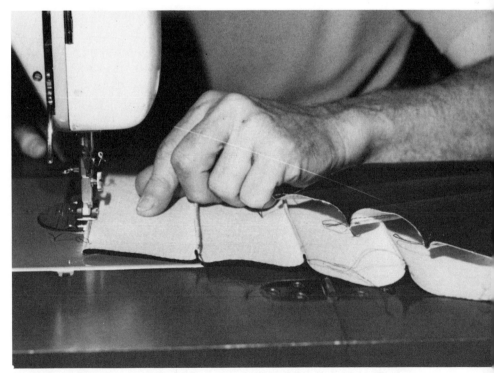

From the right side it may look like strips sewn together, but it's really one piece with seams at regular distances. Sew a second seam for reinforcement. Tie threads at end of each seam.

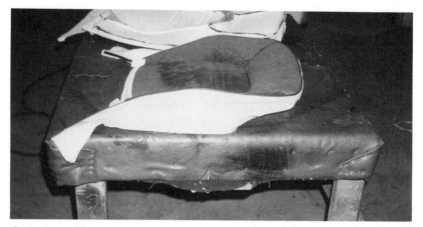

Sew pieces of seat covering together from reverse side. Welting is usually sewn where pieces join. Extra material can be trimmed if necessary to keep covering from bunching when stretched over the frame.

ments from the area to be covered if existing panels aren't complete enough to furnish a pattern.

The well into which the convertible top folds is usually lined with vinyl over fiberboard. As you'd expect, this usually curls around the edges and looks pretty ratty after a while. You may be able to recover existing panels with new vinyl. If not, cut new pieces to recover. Since these pieces may receive a lot of moisture when the rear curtain is open, it's wise to spray the fiberboard with a clear plastic spray before recovering it. This extra protection will make the panels last much longer.

Unless the seat cushions need only minor repairs, you'll find it better to remove them from the car. If the covered portion of the frames, and the back of the front seat cushion, need repair or recovering, remove the entire seat frame from the car. The seat tracks are held in place by four or more bolts that may require some soaking before they can be removed. Lift the entire seat assembly out so you can do the job properly.

With the cushions removed from the seat framework, you'll see that the job of reupholstering the seats is considerably easier than it looked when the whole thing was a unit.

If there is a folding armrest, remove it, for it must be recovered separately. It's better to remove the old upholstery material rather than try to recover the old material. Take it off carefully so you can use it as a pattern for cutting the new material. Many restorers have found it better to make a first cover of cheap muslin or duck, to be sure it fits correctly, before cutting into the more expensive leather or vinyl. In any case, cut the pattern pieces, leaving at least half an inch on each side of the seam for strength. With the pieces cut, sew them together on the reverse side so no raw seams will show. After sewing the initial seam along your pattern line you may want to sew a reinforcing seam parallel to it, about ⅛ inch from the initial seam; this second seam won't show.

When reupholstering a seat, make the top portion of the seat cushion first—that's the part you sit on. With this portion completed, sew the part that fits from the seat edge to the bottom of the cushion, which may turn under the framework. If there are separate pieces for each side of the cushion, they should be sewn to the center portion so you have one piece that will cover the front and both sides of the cushion. Mark the center of this piece, and match it with the center of the seat portion. Pin the pieces together if this will help keep the pieces in proper alignment as you

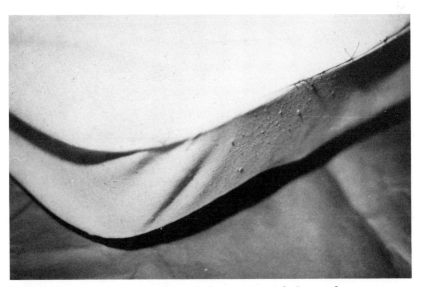

To keep from wasting expensive upholstery material, first make a test cover of muslin to be sure fit is correct. A cover of this type also protects outer cover from damage by springs.

sew. Sew slowly so you maintain an even line of stitches. If there is welting or cording between these two pieces, attach it to one piece before you sew the two together, as it will be easier to handle this way. After sewing your initial seam both directions from the center mark, sew a second reinforcing seam about ⅛ inch from it. The piece you have after these are sewn together should be stretched over the cushion to be sure it fits snugly. If not, note where changes have to be made.

On some cars, the portion of the cushion you sit on may continue to the bottom framework of the seat. On other cars there is a separate piece attached to the back edge of the cushion, which extends down to the framework. If your car has such a piece, sew it to the top portion of the cushion, then to the ends of the pieces that extend around the cushion. This gives you a cover that has all four sides and the top sewn together. You can stretch it over the cushion with little difficulty if your measurements were correct.

When spraying springs, stack them on top of each other so overspray from top springs helps cover springs beneath. It's better to spray springs before repairing or patching, then make touch-ups.

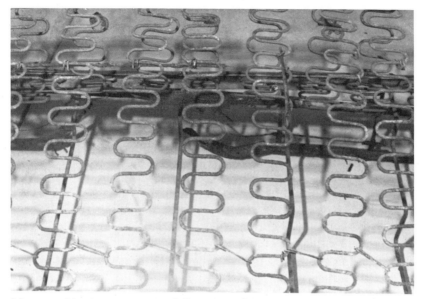

Many cushions are supported by crimped steel springs with wire clips holding springs in line. Jute or foam padding covers springs to provide comfort and prevent springs from tearing upholstery material.

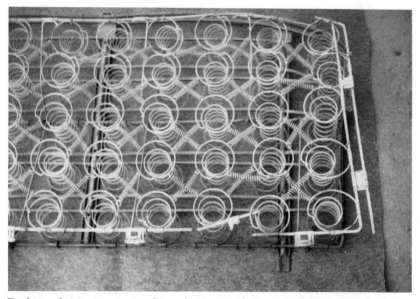

Broken edging on seat cushion frame can be repaired by welding a new piece or attaching a metal collar over pieces. Clean with wire brush and spray a coat of primer to prevent future rusting.

Before attaching this cover to the cushion, be sure the seat springs are all in place. In some cars these may be tied into position with heavy cord; in others, light wires or coil springs are stretched between the seat springs to keep them upright. Some cars use a zig-zag steel spring for support instead of coils. These springs run from the front to back of the cushion, and are attached to a steel perimeter framework. If the springs are the least bit rusty, clean them with a wire brush and spray on a coat of rust-inhibiting primer. Repair any broken springs, either by installing a good one picked up at a wrecking yard or with a metal collar over the broken parts to hold them in place.

To assure a comfortable, good-looking seat cushion, be sure the padding is in good condition. A layer of latex or plastic foam over current padding will help achieve a smooth fit. Lumpy or torn padding should be replaced before installing new upholstery.

At one time upholstery was tacked to a wooden framework at the bottom or backs of cushions. Later the wood gave way to a fiber

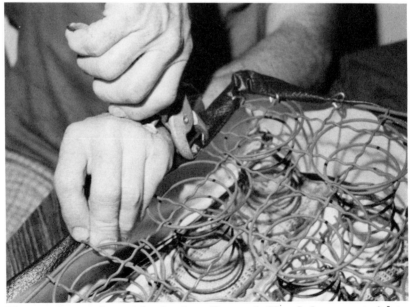

Use pig rings and special crimping pliers to hold upholstery material to framework. Use tacks to attach material to seats with wooden frames. You can cover exposed bottom with burlap or canvas.

insert in a channeled steel frame. Most upholstery is now fastened to the framework by "pig rings," the same as are pinched into the animal's snout. They're available at auto supply, hardware and farm supply stores. Purchase the special pliers used for crimping them. Occasionally you'll find a few tacks or staples used in addition to the rings. Because these rings are pierced through the upholstery, close to the outer edge, be sure you have doubled the material back and sewn a seam at the edge of the material so the rings won't pull through.

The cushions that support your back can be removed from the seat frames when the bottom cushion is out of the way. Usually a few screws hold the lower portion of the cushion to the frame. With the screws removed, the back cushion should lift out. There may be hooks along the top framework to free the cushion.

Make the pattern for the face of the cushion first, then the pattern for each side. On some cars there is also a top section. On other cars the face extends over and includes the top.

On cars with a split seat back that tilts, work on one seat back at a time. Check the pins on which the rear cushions tilt. Before final installation of new covering material, make sure the springs and framework are in good order. Use the same methods for repairing springs as outlined for the bottom seat cushions.

The material that covers the seat framework and the back of the front seat is usually stretched over a metal frame, then glued or clipped in place. On some cars there may be seams where contrasting colors and patterns are joined. Follow the decorative pattern established here, but make sure any seams that run crossway match with the corresponding seams on the adjoining panel.

Remove the old material, using as much as possible for a pattern. Draw out the pattern on the new material, leaving about an inch of material outside each line. Sew the pieces back-to-back along the seam lines. There may be as many as seven or eight pieces per seat back on cars having an indented area for extra foot room under each seat back. Sew the pieces together in such a manner that you avoid bunching too much material through the sewing machine at one time.

Be sure the padding is sufficient and is correctly positioned before installing the new covering. Stretch the material tightly to avoid wrinkles, then clip or tack it to the framework.

Molded plastic headrests can be recovered by measuring, sewing material together and stretching it over form. Glue to bottom, then hand sew seam at the bottom where it won't show.

If your car has separate headrest restraints on the front seats, you'll probably want to cover these with material matching the new upholstery. Remove the rests from the seat, and either cut the old pieces off the form to use as patterns or take enough measurements so you can make patterns for the new ones. There are many different shapes and sizes, but usually they're patterned like a miniature cushion. Because every side of the headrest shows, they're usually stitched together at the bottom, and no rings or clips are used. After making the new cover and stretching it into place, you'll have to hand sew the bottom edges together. If you made your pattern so the pieces join in the middle of the bottom, a neatly whipstitched seam won't show to detract from the car's appearance.

While you have the seat framework and track out of the car, clean the seat adjusting mechanism so it is free of all obstructions. If your car has power seats, be sure there are no bare spots on the wiring, that the motor is clean, and that cables or ratchet gears are clean and lubricated.

The procedures for covering bucket seats, used in many convertibles, are the same as for the bench-type seat with the split back. Being smaller and lighter, bucket seats are easier to handle. The same steps also apply to reupholstering the rear seats.

If you've removed the seats for reupholstering, this is the time to measure for new carpeting if needed. You may be able to use the old carpet for patterns. If not, take the measurements directly from the floor. Some cars had a separate carpet over the transmission hump, another over the tunnel in the rear compartment. Others had only a front and a rear carpet which fitted with varying degrees of smoothness over the hump and tunnel. You may also find carpeting on the riser at the bottom of the rear seat cushion.

Because carpeting may be rather expensive, and sometimes tricky to cut, try your pattern on large pieces of wrapping paper first. If they appear to fit as you want, go ahead and cut the carpeting. If you're using the loop or cut pile types with rubber backing, try to plan your cuts so you won't have a lot of loose loops or tufts that may pull out. Sew on either cording or regular carpet binding. Some cars used unbound carpets, with the edges concealed under metal plates.

If your car had rubber matting in the front or rear or both, you can use the old mat for a pattern. Check any pattern molded into the rubber matting, and make all cuts from a center line to get a good fit. Either buy carpet padding or use indoor-outdoor carpeting as padding. Don't glue padding in place. When installing padding and carpeting around pedal openings, be sure there is sufficient clearance to avoid any chance of a pedal not functioning properly. These openings will look better if they're bound.

You may be fortunate enough to have acquired a convertible that needs only minor upholstery repair and general interior detailing. If this is the case, the first step should be complete cleaning of the seats, side panels and floor.

Remove the carpets so you can give them a thorough shaking or beating. This may require removing plates at the bottoms of the doors that cover the outer edges of the carpets. Follow up with your vacuum cleaner to get all the loose dirt out of the carpet. Either use a carpet shampoo or mix your own sudsy solution of detergent and water. Use a scrub brush to give the carpets a thorough scrubbing. Rinse out the suds with clear water, then allow the carpets to dry. Be sure to shake or beat dirt out of any carpet padding or carpet underlayer.

Remove the seat cushions and either brush out the dirt and dust or use a vacuum cleaner. There are several excellent upholstery cleaning solutions from which to choose; follow the printed directions on the label, and scrub the seat cushions. For this particular cleaning you should remove all cushions. You may be surprised how well vinyl cleans, and how glossy some of the cleaning solutions will leave the seats.

With the carpets and seat cushions out of the car, use the blowing cycle on your vacuum cleaner to blow out any dust and dirt that has accumulated behind the dashboard, underneath and behind the rear cushions, and in crevices. When poking the cleaner's nozzle behind the dashboard, take care not to disconnect any of the wiring or otherwise damage instruments or accessories. After the dust has settled, use the regular vacuum to suck up the dirt.

Directions for cleaning leather upholstery are much the same as for cleaning vinyl. Many upholstery cleaning solutions claim to be equally effective on both leather and vinyl. Be sure to follow directions on the label. There are cleaning solutions made specifically for leather, as well as the old standby saddle soap. You can also use mild soap suds, if you wipe away all traces. Remember that leather can dry out and crack, so you may need to treat it with neat's-foot oil or lanolin to make it supple before trying to clean it.

When cleaning the side panels and doors, remember the object is to clean them, not soak them. Use more suds and elbow grease than water. Wipe off all traces of any cleaner, then let the panels dry. A light coat of wax will protect the upholstery and make cleaning easier next time.

At this point, with everything as clean as its going to be, determine what needs repair and to what extent, so you can plan your work. Directions on how to repair the various interior parts follow.

LEATHER REPAIR: Remove the leather cover from the cushion. This is usually attached by ring clips, tacks or staples around the bottom of the cushion. Once removed, turn the cover inside-out so you can see the extent of the damage. If only a couple of seams have split, knot the thread so it won't unravel more. If the thread has torn through the leather, you may be able to hand stitch it by sewing between the former stitch holes. If you do any hand stitching on leather, use a large curved needle with either waxed or nylon thread. Getting an exact match with leather may be difficult, as colors don't always fade evenly. If you can't locate the material you need, see if there is some leather on an inside portion or on a less visible part of the cover that could be replaced with vinyl, giving you leather to repair the seat facing.

If you have to replace one or two strips of leather on a seat facing, either hand sew them in place or sew them on a home sewing machine using a heavy needle. Be sure to leave enough leather beyond the seam so the material won't tear apart when you sit on the seat.

Frequently splits in a leather seat or panel can be patched by sewing the split or tear back together and gluing a patch on the back, or even sewing the patch in place. Small burn holes and small tears can usually be patched from the back, or sometimes sewn back together. However, you can only make these repairs if you've removed the leather cover from the cushion or panel.

Leather upholstery can be kept soft and supple by periodic treatments with neat's-foot oil, saddle soap or commercially prepared leather conditioners. Mend small tears as they appear.

There are leather dyes that may allow you to get an acceptable match if you have to substitute pieces of leather in seats and panels. Just follow the directions, after experimenting on a scrap piece until you get the hang of it. If the contrast between the original and the newly-dyed pieces is too great, consider dying the whole cushion or panel so your replacement leather won't be so obvious.

The main thing to remember when working on leather is to keep it pliable and supple. Otherwise, thread can tear through and splits may develop. Leather is only skin and can be stretched only so far before it tears.

When reinstalling a repaired piece of leather on a cushion or panel, be sure there are no sharp edges on springs, etc. that can puncture the leather. Stretch it into the proper position and anchor it firmly in place. Keep the tension even from one tack or clip to the next to avoid putting undue strain on any one piece or portion of the leather.

REPAIRING VINYL UPHOLSTERY: When repairing vinyl cushions or panels it's best to remove the material so you can make necessary repairs from the back. On doors and side panels you'll find the vinyl upholstery is glued in place. Use a flat thin blade or a putty knife to loosen the edges. With care, you can peel off the old upholstery covering the panel.

To remove the vinyl covering from seat cushions, spread the ring clips that hold the covering to the seat frame, then lift the material from the seat. On cars that have button-tufted upholstery you may find the tension on the buttons is provided by heavy cord tied to the framework. Untie this and the buttons will pull out.

Torn spots on seat cushions can sometimes be sewn back together or patched. However, the finished job will probably show repair efforts, so it's better to replace the section containing the torn material. Either secure matching material, if possible, or use a substitute acceptable to you. Before removing the damaged section, sew some stitches at the edges of the adjoining sections so the seams won't pull out, separating the other sections. Remove the damaged section and use it as a pattern for the replacement. Remember to leave extra material outside the seams to prevent raveling. Stitch the pieces together back-to-back to hide the stitches, and the excess material. Stretch the repaired cover over the cushion, but only after you've made sure there are no protruding sharp edges that might tear the cover. Secure the cover to the seat frame with ring clips. Use enough so the pressure the cushion receives as you sit or lean on it is evenly distributed.

Badly worn or torn sections of side and door panels should be cut out and replacement panels cut and stitched in place. If you can't find matching material, consider using a substitute in the same location on the opposite panel, to improve the appearance and disguise the fact that you had to substitute material.

If the thin padding between the panel and the fabric is not OK, plan on replacing it before you stretch the upholstery material into place. Lay the new covering facedown on a table or other flat work area. Coat it lightly in several spots, and apply the padding to the material. Place the fiberboard panel over the padding after you spread some glue on the side of the panel that faces the padding. Apply some glue around the edges of both the upholstery material and the fiberboard panel. When the glue is tacky, fold over the excess material onto the panel and press in place. To insure good adhesion you may want to put a board over the section. If so, put waxed paper between the board and the material so the board won't

Push metal clips from the trim strips through the slits in the material and panel, then bend them over the portion that protrudes through the panel. Upholstery material should be glued to the edge of the panel.

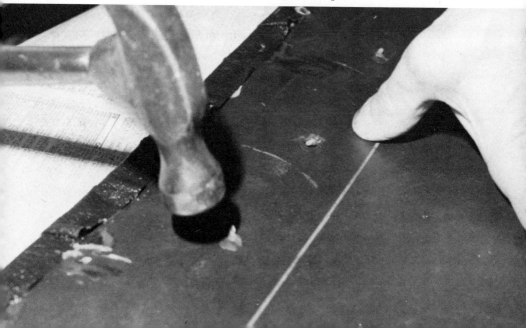

Finished panel, ready to fit. Cut holes in upholstery only after you're sure the measurements are right. Punch holes for armrest supports when panel is in place.

stick to the panel. Some restorers help keep the upholstery in position until the glue dries by looping thread or string back and forth from one edge to another. Others press a wide strip of adhesive tape over the edge of the material and panel after the glue dries.

On many cars of the 1960s and up into the 1970s, large sections if not all of the door panels and side panels are molded plastic. This allowed very fancy panels, but took them out of the reach of the beginning restorer to repair in all but the most simple cases. If your car has damaged molded panels on the doors and side, try to locate replacement panels from a wrecking yard. Remember to look at hardtop coupes, two-door sedans, even some two-door station wagons in the same make of car, as well as similar panels from other cars produced by the same parent company. Molded plastic can be successfully painted, using a paint specifically manufactured for the purpose; you may have to paint some or all of the substitute panels.

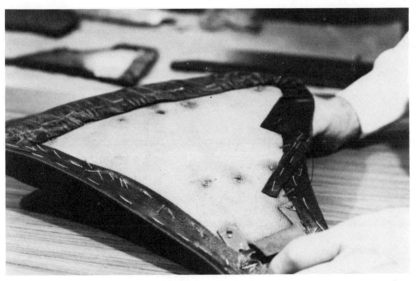

Many convertibles of the late 1960s and 1970s used molded plastic on doors and side panels. You can usually locate similar materials at trim or upholstery shops.

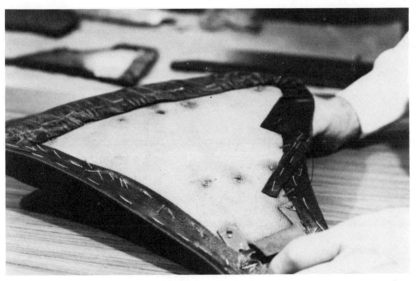

Upholstery material can be cut and stretched over armrest form. Staples hold it to form. Bracket attached to armrest fits into slot in door panel. Occasionally plated screws are used.

Armrests often take a real beating, especially the one on the driver's side as it is frequently used as a door pull. On cars only a few years old these may need repair. Methods vary, but all armrests except the ones molded on the panel can be removed. Usually screws under the armrest hold it to the inner door panel. On some cars, in addition to the screws, there are clips on the back of the armrest that slide into slots on the inner door panel.

In some cases the covering material can be repaired satisfactorily by hand stitching. In other cases the covering material must be replaced in whole or part. When working on an armrest, check the condition of the padding, for this is often in bad condition. If necessary, cut new padding. This may have to be glued in place before the covering material is installed.

REPAIRING VISORS: Visors on convertibles are often in bad shape because they've been exposed to the elements. Hot sun and plenty of water will make the vinyl covering shrink, exposing the fiberboard backing or the interior padding. To repair these, remove

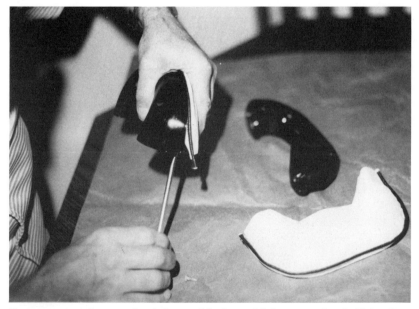

Some armrests have a plastic base with the padded top portion held in place by screws. Recover top portion and reattach to bottom half. Measure carefully for holes to line up with door.

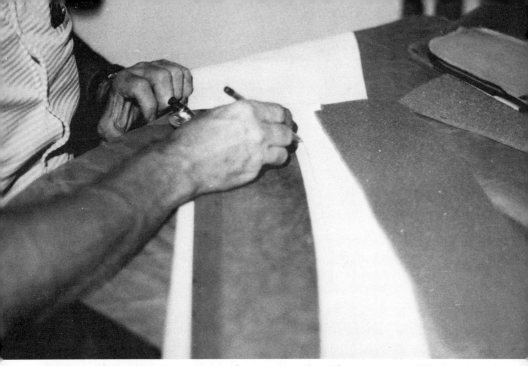

Remove old covering from visor and trace around solid center piece. Allow half an inch extra for seams. Cut light rubber padding to exact measurement and glue to each side of panel.

the visor complete with the mounting arm. If the material can't be successfully hand sewn together, make a pattern for replacement material. If the fiberboard backing has warped because of excess moisture, cut a new piece. Usually padding between backing and covering needs replacement if the covering is bad. Cut the covering materials, leaving enough material beyond the seam to avoid raveling. Place them face-to-face and sew the seam around three sides of the material. Turn the material right side out and place it over the padded backing. Fold the portions that extend over the top edge of the visor back against themselves, and run a seam as close to the edge as you can. In some cases you may need to hand sew the top edges together. Other cars have a thin metal framework around the visor edge that will hide the seam. If the visor has a small spring on the main rod holding the panel in place, be sure it is tight before you recover the panel.

CARPET REPAIRS: If the carpet is torn or is worn through in only a few places, you can probably repair it to your satisfaction. However, before making any repairs be sure to clean it

159

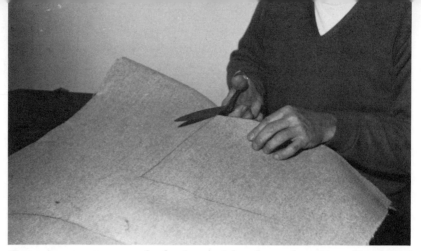

Trace carpet patterns on back of material and cut along lines. Because of the transmission hump, most cars use several small pieces of carpet rather than one or two large sections.

thoroughly. If you can locate matching carpet in an auto trim shop, you're in luck. Many times you can pick up matching carpet from a wrecked car. Remember, it doesn't necessarily have to be from a convertible or even from the same make; carpet mills supply carpets to many manufacturers. If you can't locate a piece that is what you need, consider cutting off a portion of the original carpet from under the front seat, sewing the nearest replacement you can find to that portion, and using the original for patching.

You can cut worn spots out of your carpet and cut pieces from the other carpet to fit these holes. Or you can cut out a section of the carpet and replace it with a new section. When cutting a patch piece, cut in such a manner that excess backing doesn't show. Fit the patch in place and tape the back to hold it. When the pile is brushed correctly it may not even show. You may find you'll want to sew the new piece in place; since these stitches will only be through the backing, they won't show.

Usually worn spots are below the driver's heel and to the right of the gas pedal, or wherever the driver rested his feet. You can either patch the carpet in these places or cut a scuff pad of vinyl or leather to be glued in place. Stitch around the edges if you want.

The edging or binding around some of the carpeting may be frayed and may look ratty. You should be able to find new binding at a trim shop or carpet store. If the carpeting is thick, you'll have to sew this in place by hand. A shoe repair shop might be able to stitch this for you if a carpet or trim shop won't.

160

Faded carpets can often be dyed to give a better appearance. They must first be cleaned thoroughly. To get best results from spray-on dye, plan on giving the carpet at least two coats. Spray back and forth in one direction, then back and forth at a ninety-degree angle from the first coat. In case the directions on the can don't mention it, frequently shake the can as you use it to keep the pigments mixed. Carpets should be removed from the car for dyeing, and sprayed in a well-ventilated spot. The dye dries quickly, so you will not tie up your convertible for any length of time.

To protect your carpets, you can cut and bind small "area carpets" to fit each side of the transmission hump and for the rear passenger's feet.

LUGGAGE COMPARTMENT REPAIRS: This is an area where manufacturers have cut costs in the last ten years. Not long ago luggage compartments were well finished, with finished panels on the sides and back of the rear seat and either carpet or heavy rubber matting on the floor. Now, if the sides are finished at all, flimsy cardboard is used, and this warps out of shape because of the compartment's heat. The floor covering is often poorly fitted, light-weight matting.

If you need to repair or replace the side panels, you can buy new material in large sheets from trim shops or some building supply outlets. If possible, use the old one for a pattern, or take the necessary measurements and draw your own pattern. Check to see if each side of the compartment is the same before using the same pattern for both sides. A gas tank filler pipe, or the placement of the spare wheel, may make one side different from the other. You may have to scrape off old glue from the metal panels so the new ones will stay in place. Sometimes screws are used to hold the panels in place.

If the panels are sound but only scuffed, you can spray-paint them. However, you should probably remove them from the car first to avoid inhaling the spray paint. There is a crinkle-finish spray paint that can be applied directly to the side metal panels if the car's compartment isn't lined.

You may be able to locate a replacement mat for the compartment in a wrecking yard. If not, buy either utility-weight carpeting or matting, and cut a new piece. If you do make a new one, you'll be happier with the finished product if you bind the carpeting. Matting, of course, doesn't need binding.

REFURBISHING INTERIOR TRIM ITEMS: To complete the interior restoration of your convertible, pay attention to the trim items. These are the moldings around the windshield, windows and tops of panels; the dashboard; instruments; console; door and window hardware; ashtrays, etc. Usually these items will clean satisfactorily. In some cases, however, you may need to paint them or have them rechromed.

Interior molding around the windshield usually matched the molding on the tops of doors and panels. If these are plated they may respond to a good cleaning with a strong detergent solution. Use a soft brush so you don't scratch the plating. If the plating has worn through or won't respond to cleaning, have them replated unless you want to paint them instead. If you decide to paint them, pick a color that goes well with the upholstery, and paint them all the same color. Be sure to sand them very smooth, then prime and sand again. When you've built up a good smooth prime coat, spray on a coat or two of color. A final coat of clear lacquer will protect the finish. If they have an imitation wood finish, you can send

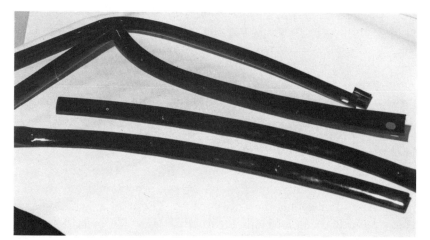

Window moldings and windshield framing can be easily refinished to any desired color. Because they're subjected to strong sunlight and all sorts of weather, give them at least two coats.

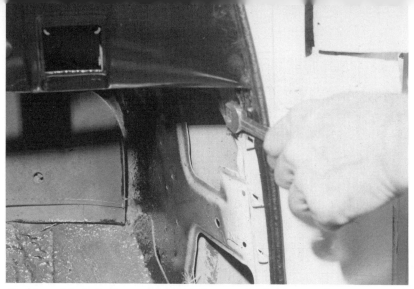

Dashboard is bolted to cowl panel. Loosen the bolts so welting can be inserted between the panel and the cowl. Tightened bolts will hold the welting in place.

them to specialists who advertise this service or can do this yourself. A general restoration book listed in the bibliography gives detailed instructions.

Window cranks, door handles, lock buttons and all interior hardware should match. If any are broken or mismatched, try to locate the correct ones. Remember that a sedan or hardtop coupe will have the same interior handles as the convertible, unless your's is a limited-edition model. You may also try to locate matching items in one of the companion makes turned out by the same parent company.

Most interior hardware is made of pot metal and can't be welded or brazed, so broken hardware must be replaced. If you have several broken or missing items and can't seem to locate replacements, consider changing the whole group for a matching set.

Interior hardware in convertibles is more apt to be dull, tarnished or even rusted because of the extra exposure to weather when the top has been lowered. Door hardware is easy to remove, as previously described, and most will look better if soaked in a strong detergent solution. A soapy scouring pad will usually remove all but the pitting marks. Rinse in clear water, and apply a light coat of wax when dry.

163

Both ashtrays looked alike before initial scouring with strong detergent and water. If fine steel wool does not remove remaining rust marks, ashtrays should be replated.

The use of plastics has increased tremendously over the years, and your convertible probably has a lot of plastic trim around the door hardware and on the dashboard. The plastic trim on the dashboard may show some deterioration and discoloration because of heat coming through the windshield. Plastic inserts that have warped out of shape can sometimes be reshaped by soaking in boiling water, then pressing flat and maintaining weight on the component until it has cooled. You might find replacement plastic parts, but they're apt to be in the same condition. Some new replacement plastic parts are now being manufactured and are advertised in various automotive magazines. Occasionally it will be necessary to repaint discolored plastic parts. This is usually best accomplished by thinning the paint and using several light coats, sanding between applications with a very fine sandpaper or emery cloth.

Dirty plastic trim parts can be cleaned with a detergent, rinsed and waxed. Often the consoles found on many bucket-seat convertibles are molded plastic or vinyl-covered metal. They will usually clean up satisfactorily. If not, the molded ones can be painted and the vinyl ones either painted or recovered. Some restorers have recovered these floor-mounted consoles (as well as

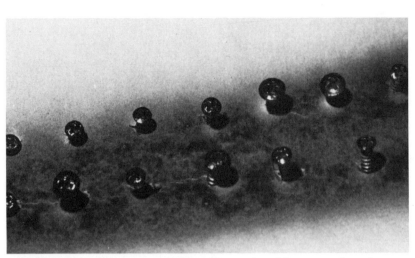

An easy way to paint screws that fit in painted moldings is to line them up through holes in a piece of cardboard, then spray back and forth.

All three plastic trim discs looked alike before two were cleaned with a strong detergent-and-water solution. These decorative plates around door and window hardware can also be painted.

A well-finished instrument panel makes a world of difference in your car's appearance. Most plated trim will clean easily. Plated parts can be coated with a thin coat of lacquer.

dashboards and window moldings) with the same type of wood-grain overlay used on station wagons. Others have found that using woodgrain adhesive-backed shelf paper makes a satisfactory job. A spray coat of clear finish will preserve it and will keep the edges from lifting.

Dirty instrument faces and dials are commonplace on many older convertibles after years of dust sift through illumination slits and around glass instrument clusters. Procedures vary by cars, of course, but many instrument clusters are held in place by two or three bolts or metal screws. Remove these and the cluster can be pulled into position to allow cleaning the dial faces. Small cotton-tipped swabs are fine for cleaning small areas. Dip in alcohol or a cleaning solvent, then wipe across the dial faces. With the glass covering the cluster loosened, clean the inside of the glass with a window spray or vinegar and water. The glass covers for individual gauges will usually come off with the snap-on rim, giving you a chance to clean both the dial face and the glass. Occasionally you'll have to reach behind the dashboard and remove an instrument's holding bracket to remove it for cleaning.

When cleaning instrument faces, be very careful not to bend or damage needles or pointers, as they're very fragile. You can usually clean the dial on the radio in the same manner. On some

166

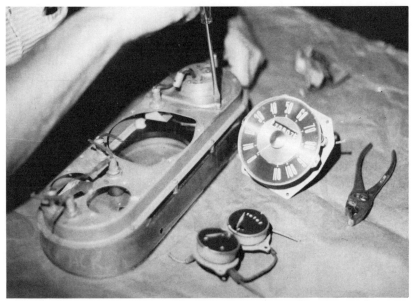

Instrument cluster can be removed for servicing. Mark wires so they can be reattached properly. Instrument faces and glass should be cleaned when you have the cluster out of the dashboard.

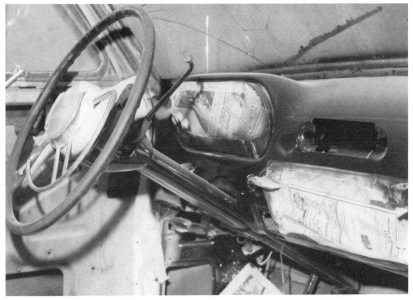

When refinishing dashboard, remove ashtrays, glove compartment door and lighter. Mask off instrument cluster, radio grille and chrome or plastic control knobs. Sand between coats.

cars you have to remove the control knobs. These are either held in place by set screws or, if pulled straight back, will come off their shaft. With the knobs off you can pull the box back and lift out the dial face.

When working around the instruments, remember that they won't stand much prying or force. The metal or plastic rims are often quite fragile, as is the thin glass covering the dial faces. You can remove the glass or plastic panel covering some types of instrument clusters from the front without having to touch the instruments at all.

When you first look into the inside of a convertible that has been abused or left out in the weather to such an extent the top is torn, the upholstery tattered and ragged, and the inside generally a mess, you may think it's beyond your capability to restore. So many people have this same opinion that many convertibles that could be restored for a moderate amount have been bypassed and consigned to wrecking yards years in advance of cars whose metal roof kept out the ravages of weather. Believe me, nothing in the interior of a convertible can't be repaired or replaced by a person with common sense and a little patience. To reassure yourself, drop in on a few trim shops and see how simple the jobs are when broken down systematically.

The time you take and the attention you give to restoring the interior of your convertible will be well invested. You'll be appreciative every time you drive the car, and you'll enjoy the favorable comments from friends. You'll also have a nice feeling knowing that as you drive and enjoy the car, it's steadily increasing in value.

7

The Roof Over Your Head

Convertibles are more fun to drive and own when the folding top is in good condition. A good top will protect your investment, helping to prevent future body and upholstery deterioration. And a good top certainly adds greatly to the appearance of your convertible. If considerable body and upholstery restoration was required because of rust damage and upholstery decay, you can appreciate the value of a good watertight top.

Perhaps the present top needs only minor repairs to give it extra years of service. Repair instructions are on the following pages. On the other hand, the present top may have deteriorated to a point where a new top is a necessity. You can buy ready-made tops for most post-World War II convertibles from a number of sources. You can also have a new top made and fitted to your car at an auto trim shop. Your third choice is to make and install the new top yourself. You can do this using a home sewing machine, thus saving a lot of money and having the pleasure of making it

A snug-fitting top that lowers and raises easily makes a convertible more fun to own and drive. Torn tops can often be satisfactorily repaired, or new tops made and fitted by the beginner.

yourself. Top materials and fittings are readily available, and not too expensive. Detailed instructions on how to make and install a new convertible roof are in this chapter.

CONVERTIBLE ROOF REPAIRS: If your checklist indicated the roof is repairable, your next step is to look more closely into damages and determine just what needs repairing. While you're at it, and to prevent damage from reoccurring, be sure to find the cause. If the damage is just a rip or a seam that had pulled apart, it may be the material was stretched too tight and something had to give as the material shrank. However, if the damage is because the folding support arms pinched the material when it was raised or lowered, you must correct this before making roof repairs. Be sure each part of the folding supports and bows works properly. There should be no protruding staples or tacks, etc. A little time examining the support arms and bows, and correcting any shortcomings, will be time well spent.

Minor tears and splits can often be sewed back in place, with a patch glued or sewed on the inside. Repaired rips lengthwise of the roof will hold together better than rips running crosswise on the fabric. Rips that run lengthwise don't have the stretch of the roof pulling at each edge. Rips across the material are constantly stretched, weakening the repair. When sewing the roof material back together to close a rip or a tear, be sure your stitches are far enough back from the edges so the thread won't pull through the

Rear window curtain of this Corvette should be refitted to remove wrinkles that distort driver's vision to the rear. Adjustment can be made in position of roof side of zippers.

Vinyl tops that have shrunk to the point where padding is exposed will have to be replaced. Ready-made replacement tops are available for most cars, or you can make the needed top.

Tear in this Buick vinyl top has been successfully repaired and hardly shows. Repair is about six inches from rear edge of quarter window. Cloth tops can be repaired too, but repairs show.

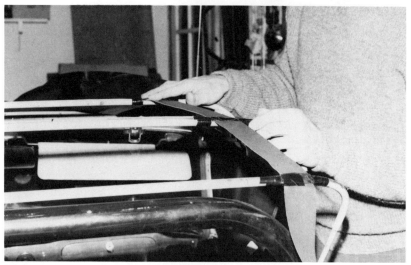

With top removed, support webs must be replaced or firmly attached to roof bows. Tape is only to keep heads of securing screws from chafing top material. Roof pads must be stretched tightly.

Vinyl roofs seem to soil easily, and mildew may form if top isn't cleaned regularly. A mild detergent-and-water solution will make cleaning the top easy. A light coat of wax helps keep it clean.

material. You'll have to decide how large a rip or tear you want to patch, depending upon the appearance of the repair.

You can replace a side or center panel if you wish. Directions are included with instructions for making a new roof. You'll have to remove the old roof to replace any panel or section other than the rear curtain-window section. In removing the old top you risk tearing the material, plus the chance that the replacement material won't match because of fading. However, many restorers have sewn new sections into existing tops and are completely satisfied with the results.

To remove an old roof, loosen the front bow so there is no tension on the fabric. Also loosen all the clips and fasteners along the edges. Remove any plated tips on weltings and moldings. Using great care, pry out the weatherstripping across the front bow. This allows you to pull out the tacks or staples holding the roof material to the front or header bow.

Remove any welting that runs across the rear from one window to another. Pull out the tacks or staples holding the material to the body. On some cars a piece of metal was inserted in a sleeve sewn to the bottom of the material, where it joined the body. Fasteners through this metal attached the top to the body, with the metal strip spreading the tension along the entire top rather than only at tack or staple points.

At this point the top fabric is still in one piece, attached only to the roof bows. Fold the material back over the first bow and pull out staples or tacks attaching the top tab to the bow. Do this one bow at a time until you reach the last bow. When you reach the last bow you may find the material is attached at both the front and the rear. And there may be an extra layer of material holding the rear curtain window in place. Pull the staples or tacks attaching this piece, too.

With the roof covering loose at all bows, you should be able to lift it off. Note at this point that the roof pads and support webbing remain with the framework. You'll need a fairly large surface on which to spread out the roof covering. If you don't have a table that is large enough, sweep a clean spot on the floor, spread some papers and work there.

After you have the measurements for the replacement panel, you can cut out the portion you plan to replace. Use a razor blade or a hooked thread cutter on the seams. If there's any graining or pattern on the material, be sure the new material is placed before cutting, so this graining or pattern will run in the right direction when cut. When cutting, remember to leave at least half an inch of extra material for seaming. Fold the material back against itself, then sew along the exact pattern mark for the entire length of the material. If you feel the material may move out of line before you sew the seam, pin the material in proper position, removing the pin just as it approaches the needle. It is along this folded-back seam that you join the new and old material. After your main seam, sew a second or reinforcing seam about ¼ inch from the first for added strength.

In the last few years convertibles have been fitted with roofs made of vinyl-covered fabric. The three main pieces comprising the main roof are bonded to each other rather than being sewn. You can buy vinyl fabric repair kits, consisting of vinyl repair patching compound, vinyl cleaner-solvent and vinyl repair paint. A heating iron with a graining head and a variable heat control switch is used to bond the material. These can be rented. In most cases the roof covering doesn't have to be removed to make these repairs.

Use a razor blade to remove frayed edges from the material. Clean the area with the vinyl-cleaner solvent to remove dirt, grease and wax. Mask off the areas around the spot to be repaired. Heat the iron to the temperature stated in the directions, usually about 300° F. Apply the vinyl patching compound with a putty knife or small spatula. Spread the compound until smooth, and clean off any excess. Run the heat iron back and forth over the area to bond the material thoroughly.

To give the graining effect of the original, run the heat iron with the graining head over the area, holding it so you're applying only light pressure and getting the graining effect you want. You can coat the entire surface with vinyl paint once it has cooled and has been properly cleaned, as instructed in the directions.

A cracked, discolored or otherwise unsatisfactory window in

the back can usually be replaced without removing the roof covering. On most cars the window is contained in a curtain that zips into place. Unzip the window and remove the fastenings to the body.

Cut the zipper out of the plastic window with shears or a razor blade. Measure and cut the replacement insert. You can buy heavy-duty clear plastic material by the yard from auto trim shops and some fabric stores. Be sure to get the heavy-duty clear plastic for best results. Sew one portion of the zipper to the plastic insert. To get the insert evenly attached to the zipper, mark the middle of the zipper and pin it to the plastic at this point. You'll find it easier to avoid bunching as you sew if you start from the pin and sew across half the top and down one side, then do the same with the other half.

On some cars the plastic insert is framed in a curtain made of top material, with the zipper sewn to the curtain and the other part of the zipper sewn to the top. In these cases you sew the plastic insert into the curtain. There may be a sleeve sewn in the curtain, into which the plastic insert fits. With the plastic insert inside the sleeve, sew one or two seams around the perimeter. No

Rear window curtains often stretch, become discolored and tear. The best solution is to obtain new clear plastic and make a new window curtain. Use a home sewing machine to sew zipper.

If top material wrinkles, as around quarter window on this T-bird, consider moving that portion of snap attached to car body to stretch material back into position. Measure position carefully.

On some convertibles the zipper is attached directly to the vinyl window, giving a larger rear window. Restorer can replace curtain by measuring and cutting new window. Sew in the zipper on a home machine.

Plastic window curtain is often attached to a flap made of roofing material. Zipper is sewn to top and edge of flap. Curtain is attached to top edge of car body and lowers into well when open.

matter how the plastic is attached, it should be sewn on the inside of the curtain or zipper so water will pass over the seam and not be retained to leak into the car.

When handling the new plastic insert, be careful not to scratch it. Cover it with paper held in place by masking tape as you work.

You'll seldom get satisfactory results painting a cloth roof. The paint will crack in time, and the material will also. Roof dyes are available to correct the situation. Use them as directed for satisfactory results. You can protect the car's finish during the dye application by an extra heavy coat of wax on the areas where the dye will drip or run. After the dye has dried, and before removing the wax, hose down the roof to rinse out the dye. Usually a coat of dye every six months will suffice if the car is not out in the bright sunlight a lot.

HOW TO MAKE A NEW ROOF: First of all, make sure the roof bows, folding support arms, operating mechanisms, pads and webbing are all in good order. If the webbing is frayed, curled at the edges or not firmly attached, this is the time to replace it. If the padding is torn, stained or lumpy, make and install new pads before starting on the new roof covering.

ROOF PADS: Take the dimensions for new roof pads from the existing ones. If these are missing, measure from the front header bow, back over each bow to the rear body line. There will be a slight indentation in each roof bow to indicate the width of the pads, normally eight to ten inches. They are double or triple layers of roof material, with a layer of cotton or foam padding sewn between the cloth. They must be thick enough to give a smooth appearance to the roof, yet thin enough so they won't make humps or ridges in the top material. They're installed on the roof bows with tacks or staples, not attached to the top covering. They should be made of material that matches the top.

Cut the top material the length you determined from the front header back to the body line. It's best to cut the material three times the width you measured, so you can fold the material over from each side. Cut polyurethane or latex padding to the same length, and to the width of the indentation in the roof bows. Cut two strips of padding for each side. Place one strip in the center portion of the triple width covering material, fold the material over

Stretch padding from front to back, attaching to roof bows. Space tacks about an inch apart for maximum strength. Use galvanized or blued tacks to prevent rusting. Set tack heads squarely on pads.

and sew a seam along the inner edge holding the foam strip in place. Place the second strip of foam over the already stitched padding, and fold the covering material back over it. Sew a seam on the outer edge, through three layers of top material and two layers of foam. Sew a seam on the other side of the padding, where until now the seam only went through two layers of covering and one layer of padding. This roof pad will give a smooth appearance to the top. To prevent the material from bunching, you may want to sew cross seams every foot.

ROOF COVERINGS: Basically, the roof consists of three large pieces of material sewn or bonded together. Since any roof you make will have to be sewn, the techniques for making a bonded roof won't be covered in these directions. The wide panel in the center usually runs from the front header bow, back across every roof bow to the rear-most bow. On some cars this center panel extends back over the rear bow down to the body line. In these cases the area for the rear curtain window is cut out of the center panel.

Each side panel should be a mirror image of the other. These run from the front header bow, along the top of the windows, and follow the back frame of the second window down to the body line. These

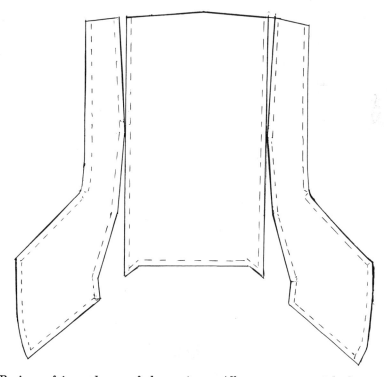

Basic roof is made up of three pieces. Allow extra material along each measurement for stitching. Sew in reinforcements to side pieces before joining side pieces to center panel.

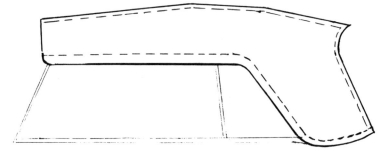

Pattern for side panel should look about like this. Dotted lines indicate material turned back for seaming. Material must follow curve of rear edge of quarter window. Measure carefully.

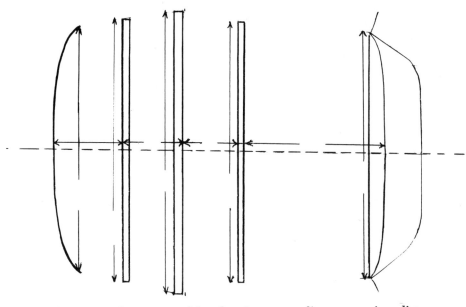

Make pattern for new roof by drawing center line, measuring distance between bows and drawing pattern. Measure from center line to edge along each roof bow, then fill in to complete needed measurements.

panels trace the curve of the body around the rear deck to the opening for the rear curtain window. Each side panel is sewn to the center panel.

Unless you have enough of the present roof to use as a pattern for these three panels, you'll have to make your own pattern.

Make a sketch showing the roof bows, and draw a center line from front to rear. Write in the dimensions on the center line from one bow to another, and from the center of each bow to the place where the center panel will join the side panels. Add half an inch on each outside edge for seaming. You now have the dimensions you need to cut the center panel.

Before you cut the material, be sure you have drawn the center line on the material and made all the measurements from the center line so any contours in the material will be even on both sides. Don't make the mistake of folding the material along the center line and attempting to cut through two thicknesses of cloth at one time. You'll end up with an incorrectly cut center panel. It's best to use tailor's chalk for marking pattern and cut lines.

After cutting the top panel and the two side panels, pin them together and lay them over the roof bows to see if they fit properly. If they do, you can finish the side panels. However, if the fit isn't just what you want, this is the time to make necessary corrections.

Most convertible tops are made with a reinforcing piece of material that follows the window line on each side panel. These pieces are usually from 1 to 1½ inches wide. After cutting them, place the strip facedown on the outside of the side panel and sew a seam close to the edge. When you unfold the pieces, the unfinished edges will be inside. Either sew binding or cording along the edge over the window to give it a finished effect. Sew another seam parallel to the window line, about an inch up from the win-

Fold material back under itself. You'll be sewing through four layers when stitching side panels to center panel. By folding lower edges in same manner, edges are reinforced when binding is sewn on.

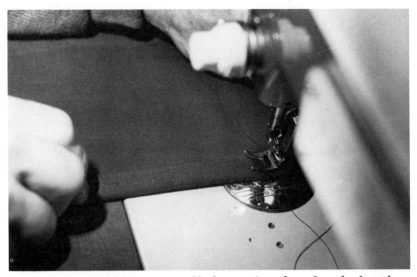

Fold top material back against itself when sewing edges. Sew slowly to keep the seam straight. Sew on binding or edging over folded material, allowing ¼ inch between seams.

dows; this attaches the other edge of the reinforcing seam to the side panels.

Pin the side panel to one side of the center panel, face-to-face, and sew a seam about ¼ inch from the edge, the length of the center panel. The side panel will be longer than the center panel, for it must reach from the rear bow to the body while the center panel stops shortly after the rear bow. Unfold the material and sew a second reinforcing seam about ¼ inch from the first seam. Place this portion of the covering back on the bows to be sure your seam was correct and that you're getting the fit you want. If you're satisfied, follow the same seaming procedures on the other side. If not, note your mistakes, mark them on the cloth, and rip out the seams to correct the errors.

At this point the edges across the front and back of these panels are still unfinished. If the roof material extends over the body metal, and the bottom edge was originally tacked or stapled to a fiber strip, you should cut it to fit, allowing about one inch extra to be turned back for seaming. If this panel was attached on the inside and covered by a trim strip or upholstery panel, make the

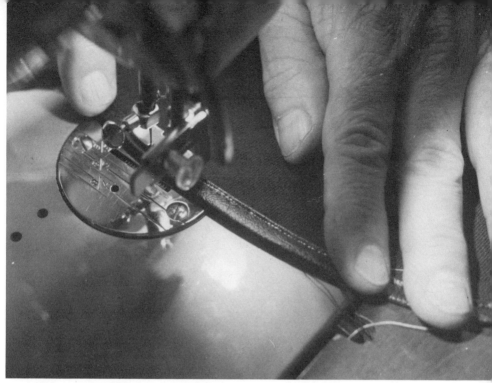

Sew binding over folded-back material to give a finished edge. On some cars the binding is a contrasting color. Sew slowly to keep seams straight.

Sew through turned-back material to inside edge of binding. When binding is folded over material, second seam goes through all layers and reinforces the seam.

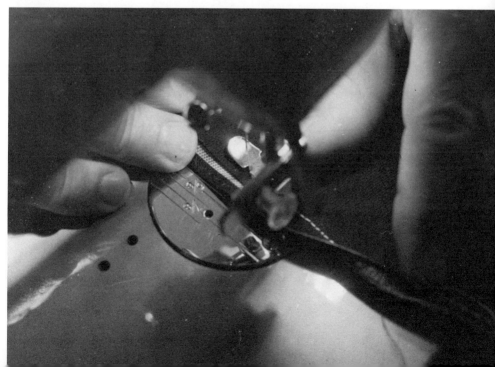

Take care to fit new top evenly to front bow, then stretch it back to rear main bow. Mark center of new top with chalk, and mate with center mark on front bow to be sure top fits evenly.

If tack strips are worn and need replacing, cut fiberboard material into half inch wide strips, glue together and attach to roof bows by pop rivets or screws. Old fan belts also work fine.

correct measurements, cut and seam. In either case, do not attach the side panels to the body at this time.

When you attach the roof covering to the bows, the center panel and the attached side panels will be tacked or stapled to the front header bow, the main rear bow and the body. The roof covering will not be attached directly to the other bows. Small tabs or sleeves sewn to the edges of the panels allow the covering to be secured to each roof bow. On some cars a sleeve is sewn to the top panel and looped over the center portion of one of the midbows. Follow the method originally used on your car.

Mark the midpoint on the rear roof bow and on the front header bow. Also mark the midpoint on the roof covering at the front and rear. Start at the rear roof bow and match the marks on the covering and bow. Tack or staple at this point. Stretch the material forward, and tack or staple the midpoint of the covering to the midpoint of the front header bow. Returning to the back bow, tack or staple (about one inch apart) each side of the midpoint for three or four inches, stretching the material as you go. Do the same

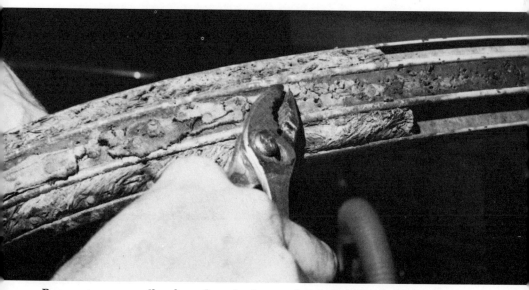

Be sure to remove all tacks and staples from tack strip before attaching new roof pads. Usually pliers will do the job, or use a screwdriver to pry up tack heads so they can be gripped by pliers.

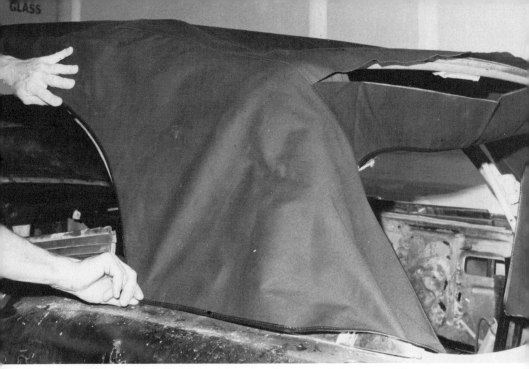

When you've sewn the new top together, stretch it over roof bows to be sure it fits around the windows before tacking it in place. When you tack, start at center of rear bow and work each way.

On cars with wrap-around wind-shields, take special care to attach top material to the front bow so it follows the curve of the windshield. Start at center and work alternately from side to side.

186

on the front bow, but stretch the material forward and sideways. Alternate attaching front and back a few inches at a time, stretching the material to avoid wrinkles. Stretch the side panels down and attach to the body. When the roof covering is in place, use welting to hide the tacks or staples, and plated tips to cover the cut ends of the welting.

It's not uncommon to find that no matter how tightly you stretched the roof there may be a few small wrinkles. These will come out once the roof is soaked a few times and shrinks a bit.

When installing the weather stripping along the front header bow, be sure it is cemented and pressed firmly in place. You should leave the new roof clamped firmly in place for at least twenty-four hours to be certain the weather stripping adheres tightly.

Cut and sew the back curtain so the top itself extends well past the opening. On most cars there is an inch or two of the center panel overlapping the outer edges of the rear curtain window. On most convertibles the rear curtain window is attached at the bottom

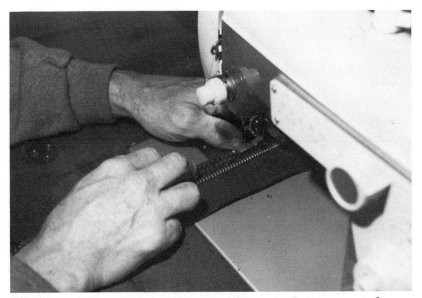

Sew zipper side to flap attached to top, other part of zipper to window or top material surrounding the window. When zippers have been joined, staple or tack bottom to tack strip in well behind the seat.

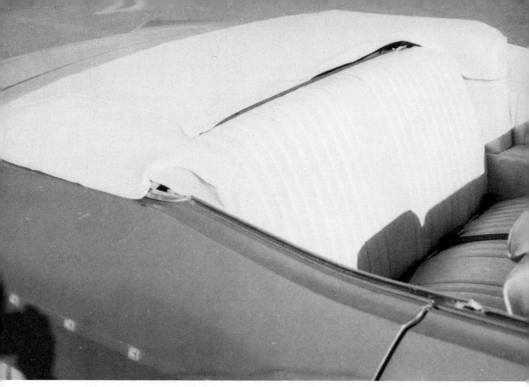

When you've finished the top, make a roof boot to protect the top when it's lowered into the well. Either match upholstery or the top. Top boot improved the looks of this car.

and held in place by one or sometimes two zippers. The attachment at the bottom allows the curtain to hang down into the roof well behind the rear seat when the curtain is open. On only a few of the earlier model convertibles will you find the curtain attached to the roof bow, opening upwards. In these cases, snaps on the roof bow, or snaps on straps between the two rear bows, hold the curtain open.

The rear curtain window should be finished and fitted with the same care as the rest of the top. Some auto trim shops and restorers use a double thickness for extra strength. Be careful, and measure exactly, so the window portion of the curtain will be positioned correctly in the opening. The window should be sewn in place before the curtain is installed in the car. On cars where the window is sewn onto the curtain rather than only to the zipper, the curtain will be attached to both the top bow and the body line. The window portion should be sewn to a small margin of top material and one-half of the zipper sewn to this material.

When you have installed the new roof, you should also make a roof boot or cover to hide the roof and keep it clean when it's folded into the storage well behind the seat. Starting at the back frame of the second window, measure around the inside of the car, across the top of the rear seat, and to the corresponding edge of the other second window. Take the outside measurements along the line where the roof joins the body. Measure the width of the side areas that conceal the folding support arms. Measure front to back from the back of the back seat to the edge of the body. With the roof folded compactly into the well, measure the height the cover must be to hide the roof. On some cars the roof boot can be a nearly flat piece of material. On others, the cover must have an upright panel two or more inches high.

When cutting the pattern, allow about one inch on each measurement for turning back and seaming. Sew a binding along the folded edge, and seam the turned-back material to prevent raveling.

If the top is operating properly, the bows and side rails should fold compactly into top well. Material should fold evenly, not bunching or getting cut by folding framework.

Use handy grommet pliers to attach snaps and grommets to roof or top boot material. Measure where grommets are to be placed, and cut or punch small hole in material. Work carefully.

Mark where the holes are to be punched for attaching the fasteners. Install a fastener at each end. With the boot snapped in place at these points, stretch the material and mark where the other portion of the fasteners are to be attached. Mark the middle spot first, then work from side to side until you have all the fasteners properly placed.

If you have enough top material left over, make an envelope to hold the boot when not in use. Store it in the well or luggage area.

You'll enjoy your convertible more if the power top operates properly, allowing you to lower and raise the top at will. If the top is properly fitted and the folding support arms are properly adjusted, the top will not be damaged when lowered or raised. The operating mechanisms are rugged and dependable, and quite easy to repair. The biggest problem is debris that finds its way into the area in which the mechanism must operate.

There are three basic variations of the power top, yet they all operate to move a pivoted main roof bow. As this main bow is moved up or down, hinged connecting side rails and roof bows move with the main bow to fold or unfold the top.

HYDRAULIC-OPERATED TOPS: The hydraulic type uses a reversible electric motor to power a rotor-type pump connected to two hydraulic cylinders. The electric pump and fluid reservoir

190

may be mounted under the hood or behind the rear seat. The action is controlled by a double-throw relay switch. A circuit breaker or fuse protects the line. The hydraulic cylinders are located below and behind the main roof bow, hidden from view by side trim panels.

To raise the top, the pump forces hydraulic fluid through the lines into the bottom of the cylinder, pushing the piston rod up. The fluid that is above the piston is forced back into the pump reservoir to be recirculated to the bottom of the cylinder. To lower the top, the fluid is forced into the top of the cylinder, forcing the piston rod down. The fluid below the piston is recirculated through the pump reservoir to the top of the cylinder.

Typical hydraulic pump mounted on fire wall. The cannister on bottom holds hydraulic fluid. Double-acting pump forces fluid through pipes to top or bottom of top-actuating cylinder.

Remove pump and disassemble it at workbench. Clean fluid inlet at bottom of pump, plus any sediment in bottom of cannister. Clean actuating solenoid and electrical connections. Check rubber hoses for leaks.

ELECTRICALLY-OPERATED TOPS: There are two types of electrically-operated tops. The older type uses reversible electric motors to drive spiral-threaded shafts through small gear cases. Upon command from the dash-mounted double-throw switch, the motors turn the shafts in one direction. These shafts turning against the gears connected to the main hinged top bow move the bow up and down. When the motor turns one way, the threaded shaft moves the main bow up and forward, the top raises and unfolds. When the switch is moved in the other position, the threaded shaft pulls the roof bow back and down, lowering the top.

A variation of this type of electrically-operated top places the motors next to the sector gear cases on the main roof bow (one on each side). Upon command, through a gear mounted on each motor shaft, the motor turns the sector gear in one direction to raise the top, in the other direction to lower it.

CABLE-OPERATED TOPS: The third type uses one reversible electric motor mounted low behind the rear seat, connected to a gear reduction unit. A flexible drive cable from each side of the gear reduction unit is connected to an actuator mounted on the main hinged roof bow. When the dash-mounted switch is turned one

192

Actuating arm and control linkage must be tight, but not to the point that the clevis pins and joints bind. Oil lightly from time to time to keep operation smooth.

way, the motor coupled to the gear reduction unit turns the cables running to the actuator, moving the hinged bow up and forward. When the switch is in the other position the process turns the cables the other way, bringing the main roof bow back and down, lowering the top framework.

To diagnose the troubles in these systems, check the following:

HYDRAULIC-OPERATED TOPS: If the top doesn't operate, check the electric motor ground. Next check the circuit breaker or fuse. Look for a bare wire causing a short circuit. Check the operation of the switch. Check the system for leaks that lower the pump pressure and allow loss of hydraulic fluid.

If the top operates slowly or binds, again check for a short circuit, a poor ground for the motor, loss of hydraulic pressure and fluid, low voltage or defective cylinders. Also check the linkage connecting the piston rods to the main bow, and the linkage and alignment of the folding support arms or frame rails.

If the top operates in one direction only, check for a defective control switch, a short circuit in the electric lines, or a bent or kinked hose.

SHAFT-DRIVEN TOP: If the top doesn't operate, check the

When replacing hydraulic lines, use two wrenches so you won't put too much strain on the coupling. Joints must be tight so fluid will not leak out and air get into the system.

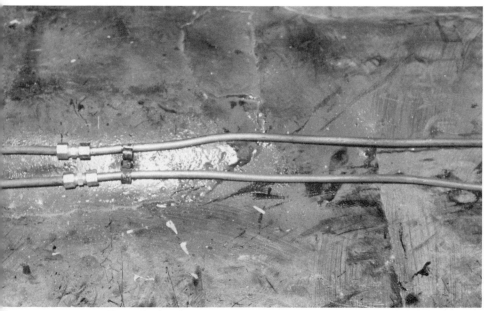

Install new hydraulic lines when old ones are rusted through. Cut old pipes squarely, file edges to remove burrs and attach couplings to joint sections.

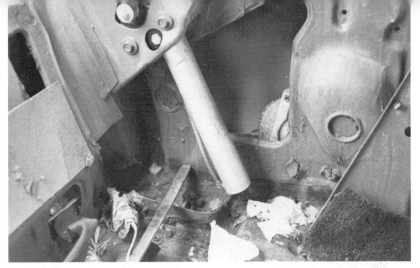

One of the main problems with power tops is debris that finds its way around the actuating mechanism, keeping arms from working properly. Dirt and rust in gear case can block action permanently.

Top-actuating motor and pump are often mounted behind the rear seat or in rear deck area below top well. Check mountings to be sure all the motion is used to move the actuating arms.

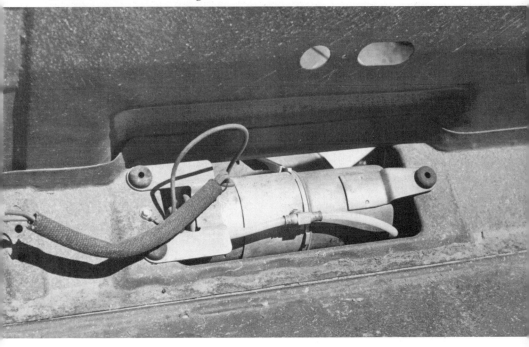

electric motor ground. Check the control switch and the circuit breaker or fuse. Check to be sure the threaded rods aren't bent and that the threads are clean. Make sure the gear cases are solidly mounted on the main roof bow. Be sure no extraneous material has become lodged in the gear case.

If the top operates slowly, binds or only operates in one direction, check the control switch. Look for damage to the threaded shafts or loose gear cases. Check for a short circuit between the motor and the switch. Also check for binding or misalignment in the folding support arms or side rails.

DIRECT-DRIVEN TOPS: As with the shaft-driven top, check the electric connections, the circuit breaker or fuse. Check for a defective motor. Make sure the small gear on the motor shaft is properly aligned with the sector gear on the roof bow. Check the bolts holding the motor, as well as the bolts holding the sector gear case to the roof bow. Make sure there is no paper or other foreign material wedged in the gear case. Check the additional items and

If latching mechanism in header bow is stuck, you may have to cut opening in bow to work on it. Clean threads. Clean and oil pivots on latching rods that fit through holes in anchor pins.

After repairing latching mechanism, cut metal patch to cover opening. Countersink screws, use filler and sand area smooth before priming and painting. Bend prongs to hold fiber tack strips in place.

conditions described for diagnosing problems with the shaft-driven top. The direct-drive top works the same way except the motors are mounted so they drive directly into the sector gear case.

CABLE-DRIVEN TOPS: If the top doesn't operate, check the ground for the motor, also the mountings for the motor. Check the circuit breaker or fuse. Check for a defective motor. Check the control switch, and look for any bare spot in the wiring. Be sure the cables are seated properly at both ends, and that there is nothing binding them. Look for something that may be binding the movement of the main hinged top bow.

If the top operates slowly, or only operates in one direction, first check the control switch. Look for a short circuit in the electric wiring. Check the actuators and the cable connections. Check for debris caught in the operating mechanisms.

You can keep the operating mechanisms performing smoothly on each type of power top by keeping the various components clean and free of extraneous materials around the mechanisms. And make sure the folding support arms are aligned. Very light oil on the clevis pin in the various support arms, as well as on the piston rods and threaded shafts, should assure smooth, trouble-free operation of the power top. Additional specific information on power tops can be found in publications listed in the bibliography at the end of this book.

8

A Coat of Many Colors

When your convertible is ready for painting, you're on the homestretch of your restoration project. Be sure these last steps are to the highest standards to protect your investment in time and materials. Any shortcuts taken in preparing the car for painting will result in less than satisfactory appearance and insidious below-the-surface deterioration, and will lessen the value of the car.

Body surfaces must be clean, dry and perfectly smooth before painting your convertible. You may not need to remove the present finish if you're sure there is no below-the-surface rust. As previously mentioned, paint blisters or cracks in the finish must be cleaned down to bare metal, the edges feathered and one or two priming coats applied.

On areas where new metal has been welded in place, the weld seam must be ground perfectly flush, any low spots filled, and the

For the best paint job, remove bumpers and grille. Sand car thoroughly, using wet or dry sandpaper in a sanding block. Prime inner areas to prevent rusting. Mask remaining plating.

Use rust-inhibiting primer on small repairs, and sand between coats. Either touch up small spots after masking the rest of the body or paint the panel, depending upon size of area and logical limits.

area sanded and primed so the patch won't show. Dents that have been pounded out must be ground smooth, filled, sanded and primed so they'll be invisible when the new finish is applied.

If you used fiberglass for patching rust-outs or for filling hard-to-reach areas, these patches must be sanded and the edges feathered, then primed and sanded. On areas where you used body putty or filler, feather the edges, sand smooth and prime to give a satisfactory appearance.

If you have to remove the old finish because of checking, cracking, etc., use either a commercial paint remover or grind it off with a power grinder. If you use a paint remover, follow the directions carefully, and be sure to rinse the area thoroughly to remove all traces from crevices and joints. If you use the grinding or wire-bristled wheel on your hand drill, be sure to get all the grinding dust out of crevices and joints.

Disconnect taillights and mark wires if there's a possibility you'll be confused when reconnecting them. Have any plating done while you're painting the car. Normally two prime coats are sufficient.

Wash the entire car to remove dirt, road film and wax. A commercial grease and wax remover can be used. Or you may want to mix your own detergent-and-water solution. In either case, the final rinse must be with clear water.

Sand the car thoroughly using wet or dry paper in a sanding block. If you choose dry sandpaper, use 240 grit on enamel, 320 grit on nitrocellulose lacquer and 320 on acrylic lacquer. If you use wet sandpaper, choose 320 grit for enamel, 360 for nitrocellulose lacquer and 400 grit for acrylic lacquer.

When using a power grinder, there are some problems to bear in mind. Use a light, even stroke, and keep the disc moving. Staying too long in one spot, or using uneven pressure, can cause burns. Leave sanding of beadings and moldings for a hand operation, for you run the risk of cutting into them with the power disc. Glazed or worn discs can cause uneven surfaces. Any metal filings or dirt on the surface will cause scratches. When changing from a coarse to a finer grit disc, cross-grind to avoid scratches. Always wear protective goggles when you use a power grinder.

For best results, remove plated moldings and trim parts. Rubber grommets should be removed to paint the metal underneath. Trim parts and accessories that you can't or don't want to remove must be masked to protect them.

When the car is completely sanded to your satisfaction, go over it with an air hose to blow all the sanding dust out of crevices and joints.

Before applying the primer coat, it's advisable to move the car out of the garage, if possible, and clean the area in which you'll be painting the car. If you can't get the car out of the painting area, be sure you've cleaned the area thoroughly, removed all the dust and dirt, and have all the parts that won't be painted thoroughly covered and masked.

Use newspapers or wrapping paper to mask areas not to be painted. Masking tape or freezer tape will hold the paper in place. If you're painting a two-tone finish, or if there are areas that are to be a different color, mask them. It's better to work from the top down. Apply the paint to the upper area, let it dry and mask it before painting the lower parts. Use care in applying masking tape on

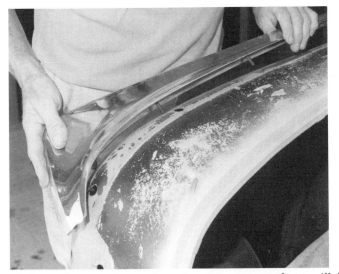

Remove bolt-on chrome trim and sand entire area so there will be no rusting metal below the new paint job. Polish or replate trim pieces before replacing them after paint has dried.

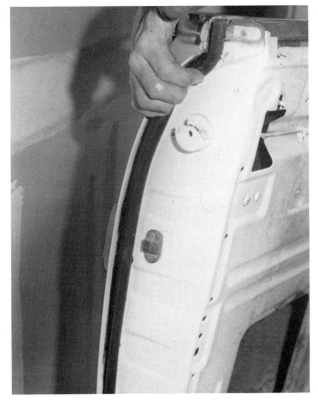

After painting the inside of door edges, hood and rear deck edges, install new rubber weather stripping and rubber door bumpers. Mask guides and parts that shouldn't be painted.

plated parts so the tape covers only the plated parts and doesn't lap over on parts to be painted.

Be sure to apply masking tape on the inside of doors to protect the upholstery. Cover areas of seat cushions, dashboard and other interior parts to protect them from spray dust.

When applying a primer coat, sprinkle a little water on the floor where you'll be walking to avoid kicking up any dust. Choose a paint sprayer that will maintain at least 30 psi (pounds per square inch pressure) and deliver at least 4 scfm (standard cubic feet per minute). The temperature in the painting area should not be below 70° F., and the area should be free of drafts. Wear a respirator-type face mask to avoid inhaling paint spray. You may want to leave a window open an inch or two, hanging a wet towel in front of the open area to allow air circulation of air but catch airborne dirt particles.

If you've never painted with a spray gun, experiment on large pieces of cardboard or scrap metal before tackling the car. The nozzle should be adjusted so the gun sprays an oval pattern about six inches in height and about two inches in width. When spraying synthetic enamels, hold the gun eight to ten inches from the surface. When spraying lacquer, hold the gun six to eight inches from the surface. If you hold the gun too far from the surface the paint will start to set before reaching the surface, and you'll have a dusty or sandy finish. If you hold the gun too close you'll have too thick a coat, which is apt to run.

Spray in a horizontal pattern, keeping the gun perpendicular to the surface at all times. Go back and forth, aiming your gun at the bottom of the previous stroke to get the overlap you need. Always start at the top of a panel or section. It may be necessary to use a vertical stroke at the edges of doors and panels for proper coverage. When spraying, it is always better to give two or more light coats rather than one heavy covering.

When you have the proper "feel" for the gun and have satisfied yourself that you know what to do, give the car a first primer coat. When this has dried thoroughly, sand it lightly with 320 grit paper. Blow out the joints and crevices with an air hose. Clean the surface carefully to remove all traces of sanding dust. And make sure the area in which you'll be spraying is still clean and free of drafts.

Spray a second coat of primer on the car. When this has dried, sand lightly with a 400 grit paper, and remove all traces of dust from the finish. In most cases, two coats of primer are sufficient. However, if for some reason you want to build up the surface, a third and fourth coat may be applied, sanding lightly between each coat. Be careful not to put on too many coats of primer as it will chip easier.

After the primer coats are sanded to your complete satisfaction, the car is ready for the color coat. Be sure the area is thoroughly clean of dirt and dust, so there'll be nothing to settle on the newly painted surface. Be sure the paint is mixed to the correct consistency for spraying, and that it has been stirred thoroughly to avoid settling.

Use the same method of handling the spray gun as for priming. Spray in even strokes, following a horizontal pattern. Press the trigger when starting the panel, and hold it until you reach the other side of the panel. At that time release the trigger, but continue the stroke for a few inches before coming back on the reverse stroke. Press the trigger as you start the reverse stroke. Keep strokes smooth and easy so you'll spray enough paint to cover the area. Keep the gun moving fast enough so you don't spray on too much paint and cause runs.

On the rear deck lid or the hood, start on the side nearest you and work toward the other side. This makes any overspray land on a dry surface rather than on a wet surface, which causes a sandy finish.

When you've completed the paint job, let the car stand until it is thoroughly dry before you remove any masking tape. Examine the finish thoroughly to see if you want to apply a second coat or touch up any areas. If you decide on a second coat, wait until the surface is thoroughly dry before lightly sanding the car or rubbing it with pumice stone. This also applies to areas where you believe a touch up is necessary.

You can either paint the wheels on the car or remove them for painting. You can't paint the inside of the wheels when they're

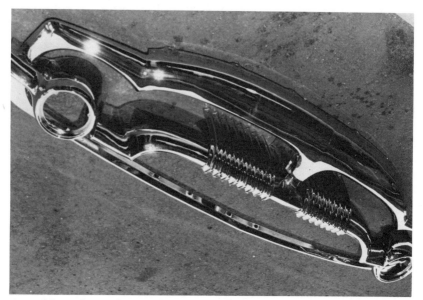

Assemble rechromed parts before installing them on your newly painted car. If bolts or nuts were replated you may have to rethread them to get the plating out of the threads.

This excellent paint job gives new life to popular Thunderbird. You're wiser to repaint a car in an original color if you ever intend to enter it in competition.

on the car. If you decide to leave the wheels on the car, mask the tires with paper and tape to avoid spray dust. If you remove the wheels for painting, clean both sides thoroughly to remove dirt, grease, etc. Sand and prime, as any other part to be painted. If you're installing new tires on the car as part of your restoration process, clean and paint the inside of the rims also. Paint the wheels before mounting the new tries. Use a soapy solution on the tire bead so the new tire will slip over the rim easily and not scar the new paint.

On two-tone paint jobs, let the first coat dry thoroughly before removing the masking tape. You may want to run a razor blade along the edge of the masking tape so it won't lift any paint while being removed.

When installing moldings and other trim parts that may have been removed for painting, handle them with care so you don't scratch the new finish. Line up clips and other attaching devices so the trim parts will fit in place easily.

If you prepared the surface properly, and took care in the priming and painting operations, you should have a finished

Careful preparation before repainting has made this Studebaker Daytona look like new. Have any necessary replating done so the finished job will have the sparkle you want.

Trim parts that alternate plating and paint, and some painted lettering, must be masked carefully if spray painted. Some restorers prefer to hand paint such parts using a small brush.

paint job of which you'll be proud. It's best to let the car sit a few days until the paint has set thoroughly before washing or waxing. On lacquer paint jobs you can rub out the finish with a light rubbing compound or pumice stone after the finish is hard. Usually twenty-four hours will suffice.

If you find any paint spray on trim or plated parts, use a little thinner to clean it off. Be careful not to allow any of the thinner to drip on the new paint. Carefully examine the inside of the doors, trunk lid and splash aprons. If you're satisfied that everything that should have been painted has been covered, you can consider the job well done.

Remember, when repainting your car you have a wide choice of colors and color schemes. You can use the original color if you like. Most major auto paint manufacturers can match original colors. You may want to choose a different color, yet one that was originally offered by the manufacturer. Or you may want an entirely different color, not originally offered. Many restorers choose a color that will go well with new upholstery they've installed. Others may dream up a color combination to suit their own fancy. Unless you intend to show the car in serious competition, where an original color would mean more points, paint the car whatever color you wish.

208

9

Keep America Beautiful

After the time and money you've spent to restore your convertible, there are some simple steps you should follow to keep it in showroom condition, continually appreciating in value. You should protect it as you would any other asset.

First of all, park the car in a secure place. Old cars, especially restored ones, are attractive to thieves. Keep the car locked so children can't play in it. You should also protect it from the weather, as by now you know the damage that continued exposure to weather can do to convertibles.

Keep the car clean. Wash and wax it regularly. Rinse dirt from under fenders, rocker panels, bumpers, etc. to keep it from accumulating, inviting moisture. Sweep and vacuum the interior regularly. If you put in new wool carpeting, treat it to prevent moth damage. Be sure there are no openings in the body that will allow field mice to enter and make a nest; they love a seldom-used car as a nesting spot, and they are very destructive. You may need to re-

Popular Chevrolet Impala can be enjoyed for years if owner will take care of minor repairs and blemishes as they appear.

move the carpets from time to time to remove dirt that accumulates underneath.

Clean the seat cushions regularly, especially after anything is spilled on them. There are fine vinyl upholstery cleaners available; just follow the directions. You can also clean vinyl easily with a mild solution of detergent and water. Rinse with clear water, and give a light coat of wax. If your car has leather upholstery, either use a cleaner made especially for leather or clean it with saddle soap. Occasionally apply a light coat of neat's-foot oil to keep the leather supple and to prevent cracking.

Upholstery on doors and side panels should be cleaned regularly. Use the same cleaning agents and methods you use on seat cushions. When cleaning side panels, clean and wax the garnish moldings and the dashboard. Tighten the screws in these components as well as in the sill plates.

If there are any signs of leaks, determine the sources and correct them. You can sprinkle the car with a hose to see if water leaks in. If after you've driven on a dusty road you find shafts of dust in the car, determine the source. When searching out leaks, remember that water will seek the lowest level, so the leak may be some distance away from a puddle.

Check the drain holes in bottoms of doors, side panels, rocker panels and deck lids. Lift the spare tire out from time to time to be

There is much enjoyable driving ahead in this intermediate size Chevrolet, which will hold its value for many years.

The large, luxurious 1958 Buick Limited has long since reached its lowest price. With tender loving care, price will continually go up.

Distinctive rear styling of Cadillac will keep it a favorite and contribute to car's increase in value as years roll by.

Massive front-end styling and wrap-around windshield of 1955 Cadillac convertible has found favor with many restorers.

sure the drain hole in the bottom of the tire well is open. Clean the luggage compartment regularly, and look for leaks. Lift out the floor covering and sweep or vacuum accumulated dirt.

Pay particular attention to the condition of the weather stripping around doors, vent windows, deck lid openings, etc. Cement into place stripping that comes loose. Lubricate with silicone spray to keep weather stripping resilient. Replace any stripping that has lost its resiliency and started to crack.

Replace any glass that becomes cracked, fogged or chipped. Use only clear water or a window spray on the plastic rear window.

The 1964 Buick Electra 225 convertible is about the largest car you'll find. A capable performer, this high-quality convertible is increasing rapidly in value.

Low initial production and fantastic performance will keep the value of 1960 Corvettes increasing as the years roll by.

The 1964 Thunderbird convertible incorporated many styling and mechanical features that will keep it in demand and force prices upward.

Never use an abrasive. Use a chrome cleaner and polish on chromium plating, mild detergent-and-water solution on the other plated parts. A light coat of wax will protect plated parts.

Tighten screws in the top assembly and keep folding support arms and side rails aligned. Use light oil or powdered graphite on joints and clevis pins. Keep the areas in which the top lowering/raising mechanism is located clear of gum wrappers, cigarette butts and other odds and ends that have a habit of working their way into the mechanism and really fouling things up. Check the wiring connections on these parts regularly.

The best way to preserve a convertible top is to keep it clean. Use a whisk broom to clean along the welting and seams. Vacuum cloth tops regularly. Clean vinyl-coated fabrics with a mild solution of detergent and water, and occasionally apply a light coat of wax. Check fasteners around the rear quarter panels as well as the fasteners on the front header bow. Check the roof pads and webbing to be sure they're securely in place and that no tacks or staples are pulling loose. Examine the seam binding and welting. If any threads are pulling loose, hand stitch that area to prevent the seam or binding from pulling apart.

To protect the paint job, check the hood alignment to avoid chafing the paint at the cowl. Check alignment of the doors to avoid marks on adjoining panels from misalignment. Check alignment of the rear deck lid for the same reason. Use a little powdered graphite in locks and on door and lid latches.

America's only hardtop convertible, the Ford Fairlane 500 featured a long rear deck to hold the roof. These comparatively rare models are a good investment.

Chrysler's good looks were coupled with high performance and quality construction, keeping rare convertible models in demand.

Style has kept Pontiac top sellers for years. LeMans featured combination grille and front bumper. These models will become collectors' cars.

Convertibles as good-looking as this Oldsmobile deserve to be preserved for future enjoyment. They'll hold their value for years, and will start increasing in value after that.

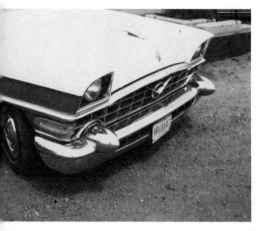

Distinctive front end styling of this 1956 model, the last real Packard, can be enjoyed in years to come as restorers keep these valuable cars running.

Fast disappearing from the automotive scene, 1960 Lincoln Continentals are worth restoring. High quality and massive styling set the car's value.

Well-restored convertibles like this 1965 Studebaker Lark Daytona will help keep America beautiful. Because of scarcity, it will be a beautiful investment too.

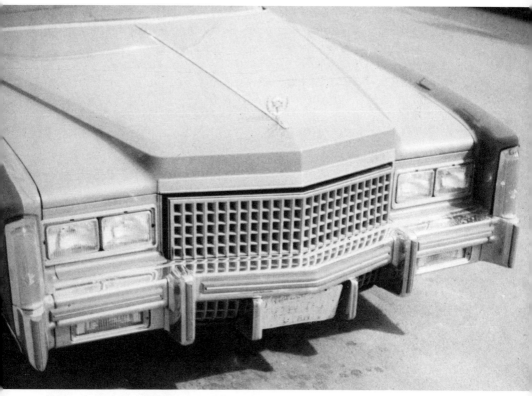

Squared-off front design of Cadillac's last convertible should be preserved for years as these fabulous cars find their niche in history.

You can protect bumpers, grilles and other heavily plated parts by a thorough washing and a light coat of wax. Usually marks on bumpers from minor scrapes will clean off by scrubbing with a medium-bristled brush. You can keep rim rings, wheel covers and hubcaps looking like new by washing with a mild detergent solution and, after rinsing, applying a light coat of wax. White sidewalls will come clean by scrubbing with a cleaner made for that purpose, or with a solution of detergent and water. A fairly stiff-bristled brush will do the job. Unless the rubber is gouged, it will come clean.

The best and easiest way to keep your restored convertible in tiptop shape is by regularly attending to the items mentioned in this chapter. If you catch the little things as they happen, you can correct them before they become major problems. Mend small tears in the upholstery and top, cement loose weather stripping, make minor adjustments as soon as you notice they're necessary. Repair minor dents and dings, and touch up the areas to prevent rust and deterioration.

By all means, join one of the many car clubs, preferably a national club dedicated to your marque or class of car. The publications issued by these clubs are very interesting, offering a valuable source of information and replacement parts. If there is a local chapter of the club, join this and participate in the many club activities. These are a fine source of parts and information, and many have certain tools and literature available on a loaner or rental basis. Many clubs have enjoyable social programs too. Subscribe to one or more of the national car magazines; you'll find them enjoyable and interesting, and they will keep you up-to-date on prices of cars like yours.

Drive and enjoy your convertible, smug in the knowledge that as every month passes the car is worth more.

Checklist A

MAKE _____ MODEL _____ YEAR _____

OVERALL MECHANICAL CONDITION _____

_____

_____

ASKING   FINAL

PRICE _____ PRICE _____

EXTERIOR

1. *Fenders*

	BEYOND REPAIR	BAD	AVERAGE	OK	COMMENTS
F.R.	_____	_____	_____	_____	_____
F.L.	_____	_____	_____	_____	_____
R.R.	_____	_____	_____	_____	_____
R.L.	_____	_____	_____	_____	_____

2. *Rocker Panels*

	BEYOND REPAIR	BAD	AVERAGE	OK	COMMENTS
LEFT					
RIGHT					

3. *Cowl*

	BEYOND REPAIR	BAD	AVERAGE	OK	COMMENTS
LEFT					
RIGHT					

4. *Doors*

	BEYOND REPAIR	BAD	AVERAGE	OK	COMMENTS
LEFT					
RIGHT					

5. *Body Panels*

	BEYOND REPAIR	BAD	AVERAGE	OK	COMMENTS
LEFT					
RIGHT					

6. *Deck Lid*

BEYOND REPAIR	BAD	AVERAGE	OK	COMMENTS

7. *Panel Below Deck Lid*

BEYOND REPAIR	BAD	AVERAGE	OK	COMMENTS

8. *Hood*

BEYOND REPAIR	BAD	AVERAGE	OK	COMMENTS

9. *Paint*

BEYOND REPAIR	BAD	AVERAGE	OK	COMMENTS

10. *Chrome Plating*

BEYOND REPAIR	BAD	AVERAGE	OK	COMMENTS

11. *Glass*

BEYOND REPAIR	BAD	AVERAGE	OK	COMMENTS

12. *Roof*

	BEYOND REPAIR	BAD	AVERAGE	OK	COMMENTS
FABRIC					
PADS					
BOWS					
REAR WINDOW					
MECHANISM					
OTHER					

13. *Summary*

_____

_____

INTERIOR

1. *Floors*

BEYOND REPAIR	BAD	AVERAGE	OK	COMMENTS

2. *Structural Supports*

BEYOND REPAIR	BAD	AVERAGE	OK	COMMENTS

3. *Top and Top Bows*

	BEYOND REPAIR	BAD	AVERAGE	OK	COMMENTS
RAILS					
HARDWARE					
STORAGE WELL					

4. *Upholstery*

	BEYOND REPAIR	BAD	AVERAGE	OK	COMMENTS
F. SEAT					
R. SEAT					
R. DOOR					
L. DOOR					
R. PANEL					
L. PANEL					

5. *Carpets*

	BEYOND REPAIR	BAD	AVERAGE	OK	COMMENTS
FRONT					
REAR					
KICK PADS					
REAR DECK					

6. *Dashboard*

BEYOND REPAIR	BAD	AVERAGE	OK	COMMENTS

7. *Accessories*

BEYOND REPAIR	BAD	AVERAGE	OK	COMMENTS

8. *Interior Hardware*

	BEYOND REPAIR	BAD	AVERAGE	OK	COMMENTS
DOORS	‒‒‒‒‒	‒‒‒‒‒	‒‒‒‒‒	‒‒‒‒‒	‒‒‒‒‒‒‒‒‒
WINDOWS	‒‒‒‒‒	‒‒‒‒‒	‒‒‒‒‒	‒‒‒‒‒	‒‒‒‒‒‒‒‒‒
DASH	‒‒‒‒‒	‒‒‒‒‒	‒‒‒‒‒	‒‒‒‒‒	‒‒‒‒‒‒‒‒‒

9. *Summary* ‒‒‒‒‒‒‒‒‒‒‒‒‒‒‒‒‒‒‒‒‒‒‒‒‒‒‒‒‒‒‒‒‒‒‒‒‒‒‒

‒‒‒

Checklist B

List the estimated time and cost of materials you feel will be necessary to repair or replace the items from Checklist A.

EXTERIOR

1. *Fenders*

	EST. TIME	MATERIALS	ACTUAL
F.R.			
F.L.			
R.R.			
R.L.			

2. *Grille, Lights, Brightwork, Trim, Etc.*

EST. TIME	MATERIALS	ACTUAL

3. *Rocker Panels*

	EST. TIME	MATERIALS	ACTUAL
RIGHT			
LEFT			

4. *Doors*

	EST. TIME	MATERIALS	ACTUAL
RIGHT			
LEFT			

5. *Cowl*

	EST. TIME	MATERIALS	ACTUAL
RIGHT			
LEFT			

6. *Body Panels*

	EST. TIME	MATERIALS	ACTUAL
RIGHT			
LEFT			

7. *Deck Lid*

EST. TIME	MATERIALS	ACTUAL

8. *Roof*

	EST. TIME	MATERIALS	ACTUAL
FABRIC			
PADS			

	EST. TIME	MATERIALS	ACTUAL
BOWS			
REAR WINDOW			
MECHANISM			
OTHER			

9. *Paint*

INTERIOR

1. *Upholstery*

	EST. TIME	MATERIALS	ACTUAL
F. SEAT			
R.SEAT			
R. DOOR			
L. DOOR			
R. QTR.			
L. QTR.			

2. *Carpets*

	EST. TIME	MATERIALS	ACTUAL
FRONT			
REAR			
KICK PADS			
REAR DECK			

3. *Top*

	EST. TIME	MATERIALS	ACTUAL
SIDE RAILS	_____	_____	_____
HARDWARE	_____	_____	_____
STORAGE WELL	_____	_____	_____

4. *Interior Hardware*

	EST. TIME	MATERIALS	ACTUAL
DOORS	_____	_____	_____
WINDOWS	_____	_____	_____
DASH	_____	_____	_____

5. *Miscellaneous*

	EST. TIME	MATERIALS	ACTUAL
_____			
_____			
_____			

Bibliography

MECHANICAL REPAIRS:

Chilton's Auto Repair Manual, 1940–1953; 1954–1963; 1964–1971; 1972, 1973, 1974, 1975, 1977. Radnor, Pa.: Chilton.

AUTOMATIC TRANSMISSION REPAIRS:

Automatic Transmission, Mathias F. Brejcha. Chicago: American Technical Society, 1974.

Automatic Transmissions, Walter B. Larew. Radnor, Pa.: Chilton, 1966.

AIR CONDITIONING REPAIR:

Chilton's Auto Air Conditioning Manual. Radnor, Pa.: Chilton, 1976.

Automotive Air Conditioning, AG Lithgow, San Diego, Cal.: National Automotive Service, Inc.

GENERAL AUTOMOTIVE RESTORATION:

Chilton's Auto Restoration Guide, Burt Mills. Radnor, Pa: Chilton, 1975.

LEATHER WORK:

Leather Work for the Restorer, Butler. Arcadia, Calif.: Post Motor Books, 1969.

PAINTING:

Car Spraying Made Easy, Jaspar. Birkenhead, England.

PLATING:

Electro-plating for the Amateur, L. Waburton. New York: International Pubns. Service.

SHEET STEEL:

Automobile Sheet Metal Repair, Robert L. Sargent. Radnor, Pa.: Chilton, 1969.

WELDING:

Modern Welding, Andrew D. Althouse, Turnquist and Bowditch. South Holland, Ill.: Goodheart-Wilcox, 1976.

ADDITIONAL INFORMATION:

Additional specific information can be found in the catalogs published by the following:

CARBOOKS, INC., 181 Glen Avenue, Sea Cliff, New York 11579

CLASSIC MOTORBOOKS, P.O. Box 1/FO1, Osceola, Wisconsin 54020

CRANK'EN'HOPE PUBLICATIONS, Box 90H, 450 Maple Avenue, Blairsville, Pennsylvania 15717

Sales literature on most U.S.-made cars is available from: Tom Bonsall, P.O. Box 7298, Arlington, Virginia 22207

Index

Page numbers in *italics* are those on which illustrations appear.